RAISING KIDS WHO READ

RAISING KIDS WHO READ

WHAT PARENTS AND TEACHERS CAN DO

DANIEL T. WILLINGHAM

A Wiley Brand

Cover design by Wiley

Baby reading © Jose Manuel Gelpi diaz | Thinkstock
Kids reading © Jacek Chabraszewski | Thinkstock
Girl reading © Stuart Miles | Thinkstock

Published by Jossey-Bass
A Wiley Brand
One Montgomery Street, Suite 1200, San Francisco, CA 94104–4594—www.josseybass.com
/highereducation

Jossey-Bass books and products are available through most bookstores. To contact Jossey-Bass
directly call our Customer Care Department within the U.S. at 800-956-7739, outside the U.S.
at 317-572-3986, or fax 317-572-4002.

Wiley publishes in a variety of print and electronic formats and by print-on-demand. Some
material included with standard print versions of this book may not be included in e-books or in
print-on-demand. If this book refers to media such as a CD or DVD that is not included in the
version you purchased, you may download this material at http://booksupport.wiley.com. For
more information about Wiley products, visit www.wiley.com.

Library of Congress Cataloging-in-Publication Data

Library of Congress Cataloging-in-Publication Data has been applied for and is on file with the
Library of Congress.

ISBN 978-1-118-76972-0 (cloth); ISBN 978-1-118-91150-1 (ebk.);
ISBN 978-1-118-91158-7 (ebk.)

Printed in the United States of America
FIRST EDITION
HB Printing   10 9 8 7 6 5 4 3 2 1

CONTENTS

For Trisha

ABOUT THE AUTHOR

Daniel Willingham is professor of psychology at the University of Virginia, where he has taught since 1992. Until about 2000, his research focused solely on the brain basis of learning and memory. Today, all of his research concerns the application of cognitive psychology to K–16 education. He writes the "Ask the Cognitive Scientist" column for *American Educator* magazine and is the author of *Why Don't Students Like School?* (Jossey-Bass, 2009) and *When Can You Trust the Experts?* (Jossey-Bass, 2012). His writing on education has appeared in thirteen languages. He earned his BA from Duke University and his PhD in cognitive psychology from Harvard University. His website is www.danielwillingham.com.

ACKNOWLEDGMENTS

I received useful feedback from Helen Alston, Karin Chenoweth, Tracy Gallagher, Fred Greenewalt, Lisa Guernsey, Michael Kamil, Margie McAneny, Mike McKenna, and Steve Straight. Special thanks to Lauren Goldberg, Kristen Turner, and Shannon Wendling and to seven anonymous reviewers, each of whom provided detailed comments on the entire manuscript. Gail Lovette generously offered consultation throughout this project. David Dobolyi did yeoman's work on the survey reported in the Introduction, and Anne Carlyle Lindsay created many of the figures. My thanks, as ever, to Esmond Harmsworth for his unfailing support and sound advice, and to Margie McAneny, who took special care with this project. Most of all, I thank Trisha Thompson-Willingham, my parenting lodestar; her wisdom informs much of the approach outlined in this book.

Introduction

Have Fun, Start Now

We're going to start this book with a quick thought experiment. Suppose you have a teenaged child. (If you actually do, so much the better.) Surveys show that the typical teen has about five hours of leisure time each weekday. How would you like your teenager to spend those five hours? To provide a little structure, I'll give you six categories of activities among which the time could be allocated. (Note that with six categories, equal time to each activity is fifty minutes.)

Relaxing/thinking	__ minutes
Playing video games/using a computer	__ minutes
Reading	__ minutes
Socializing	__ minutes
Watching television	__ minutes
Playing sports	__ minutes

Have your answers? You can compare them to the results of a survey I conducted of three hundred American adults. I've also depicted the *actual* number of minutes that teens spend on each activity, according to the national American Time Use Survey (figure I.1). For reading, the hoped-for amount among my respondents was 75 minutes. The actual time American teenagers spend reading is 6 minutes.

The purpose of this book is simple. Parents want kids to read. Most kids don't. What can parents do about that?

Of course, some kids do grow up as readers. The numbers in figure I.1 are a little deceptive because they are averages; it's not that each teenager goes home from school, reads for six minutes, and then puts the book

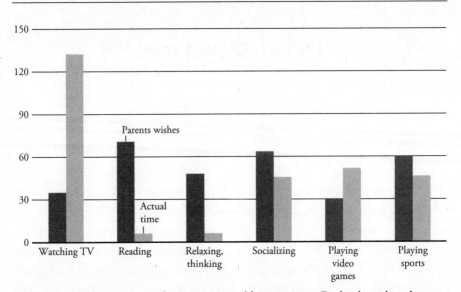

Figure I.1. Wishes versus reality in teenagers' leisure time. Darker bars show how our survey respondents hoped teenagers would spend their leisure time. Lighter bars show actual leisure time spent, according to the American Time Use Survey.
Source: © Daniel Willingham.

down. Most kids don't read at all, and a few read quite a lot. Can the parents of those readers provide us with any guidance?

In my experience, most of those parents have little idea of how their kids ended up as readers. A conversation I had with an editor at the *New York Times* is typical. I mentioned I was working on this book, and he told me that his eighth grader was the kind of kid who had to be reminded to step outside every now and then to get a little fresh air, so devoted was she to whatever book she was reading. When I asked what he and his wife had done to foster this passion, he laughed heartily and said, "Not a damn thing."

Now, almost certainly he *has* done things that prompted his child to read. He's a newspaper editor, for crying out loud. He probably read to his daughter when she was little, his house is probably filled with books, and so on. I'm sure he'd agree. What I think he meant by "not a damn thing" was, "We didn't plan it." Parents who raise readers don't do things that look especially academic. They aren't tiger parents, breaking out flash cards when their baby turns twelve months and starting handwriting drills at twenty-four months. Such measures are not only unnecessary, they would undercut a crucial positive message that these parents consistently send: reading brings pleasure. Most of what I suggest in this book is in the spirit of emulating nontiger parents, and I encapsulate it in this simple principle: *Have fun.*

Another principle guides the advice in this book: *Start now.* Parents tend to think about the different aspects of reading as each comes up in school. They think about decoding (learning the sounds that letters make) in kindergarten, when it's first taught. Parents don't think about reading comprehension at that point, because it's not emphasized in kindergarten. If kids can accurately say aloud the words on the page, they are "reading." But by around the fourth grade, most kids decode pretty well, and suddenly the expectation for comprehension ratchets up. At the same time, the material they are asked to read gets more complex. The result is that some kids who learned to decode just fine have trouble when they hit the higher comprehension demands in fourth grade. And that's when their parents start to wonder how they can support reading comprehension.

Parents often don't think about reading motivation until middle school. Almost all children like to read in the early elementary years. They like it at school, and they like it at home. But research shows that their attitudes toward reading get more negative with each passing year. It's easy for parents to overlook this change because children's lives get so much busier as they move through elementary school; they spend more time with friends, perhaps they take up an instrument or sport, and so on. When puberty hits, their interest in reading really bottoms out. A parent now realizes that her child never willingly reads and starts to think about how to motivate reading.

At these three crisis points that prompt parents to think about reading, we see the three footings for a reading foundation. If you want to raise a reader, your child must decode easily, comprehend what he reads, and be motivated to read.

How, then, to ensure that these three desiderata are in place?

Obviously, hoping for the best and reacting if a problem becomes manifest is not the best strategy. It's easier to avoid problems than to correct them. But reading presents a peculiar challenge because experiences that seem unimportant are actually crucial to building knowledge that will aid reading. Even stranger, this knowledge may be acquired months or even years before it's needed. It lies dormant until the child hits the right stage of reading development, and then abruptly it becomes relevant. That's why the second guiding principle of this book is, *Start now*. "Start now" means attending to decoding, comprehension, and motivation early in life—as early as infancy. But it also means that action to support your child's reading never comes too late, even if your child is older and you've done nothing until now. Just start.

These three foundations also provide an organizing principle for this book. In the first chapter, you'll get some of the science of reading under your belt. How do children learn to decode? What is the mechanism by which they understand what they read, or don't? And why are some children motivated to read, whereas others are not? The remainder of the book is separated into three parts, divided by age: birth through preschool, kindergarten through second grade, and third grade and beyond. Within each part, separate chapters are devoted to how you can support decoding, comprehension, and motivation at that age. I will discuss not only what you can do at home, but what you can expect will be happening in your child's classroom.

That said, if you want to raise a reader, you should not rely much on your child's school. That's not a criticism of schools but rather a reflection of what this enterprise is all about. Let me put it this way. You've got this book in your hands, so I'm assuming you're at least somewhat interested in your child being a leisure reader. Why?

Some answers to this question are grounded in practical concerns. Reading during your leisure time makes you smarter. Leisure readers grow up to get better jobs and make more money. Readers are better informed about current events, and so make better citizens.

These motives are not unreasonable, but they are not my motives. If I found out tomorrow that the research was flawed and that reading doesn't makes you smarter, I would still want my kids to read. I want them to read because I think reading offers experiences otherwise unavailable. There are other ways to learn, other ways to empathize with our fellow human beings, other ways to appreciate beauty; but the texture of these experiences is different when we read. I want my children to experience it. Thus, for me, reading is a value. It's a value—like loving my country or revering honesty. It's this status as a value that prompts to me to say, "Don't expect the schools to do the job for you."

I'm reminded of a parent I know who was dismayed when his child announced that she was marrying someone of a different faith. Her father asked how the children would be raised, and she made it plain she was not much concerned one way or the other. Although he and his wife had not made religious identity much of a priority at home, he was nevertheless surprised and hurt by his daughter's decision. "I can't understand it," he told me. "We sent her to Sunday school every week." He had subcontracted the development of this core value.

If you want your child to value reading, schools can help, but you, the parent, have the greater influence and bear the greater responsibility. You can't just talk about what a good idea reading is. Your child needs to observe that reading matters to you, that you live like a reader. *Raising Kids Who Read* aims to show you in some detail how to do that and with a sensibility that embodies two principles: we have fun, and we start now.

NOTES

"makes you smarter": Ritchie, Bates, and Plomin (2014).

"better jobs and make more money": Card (1999); Moffitt and Wartella (1991).

"maker better citizens": Bennett, Rhine, and Flickinger (2000).

1

The Science of Reading

Scientists have learned a lot about the mental machinery that supports reading, and this research base inspires much of what I suggest you do throughout this book. So we need to get the basics of these scientific findings straight. I'll introduce scientific findings about reading as they become relevant, but this chapter starts with three foundational principles, to which we'll return again and again: (1) the sounds that letters make (not their shape) pose the real challenge as children learn to read print, (2) comprehending what we read depends mostly on our general knowledge about the topic, and (3) the key to motivation lies in getting kids to read even when they aren't motivated to do so.

The Role of Sound in Reading

We think of reading as a silent activity—consider a hushed library—but sound in fact lies at its core. Print is mostly a code for sound. English uses some symbols that carry meaning directly; for example, "$" means dollars, "@" means at, and ":-)" means smiling. But "bag" is not a symbol for a paper sack. It's three letters, each of which signifies a sound; together, the sounds signify a spoken word. English is not alone in using a sound-based writing system. All written languages have some number of symbols that carry meaning, but the workhorse of communication is a sound-based code.

Because writing uses visual symbols that signify sound, children who are learning to read must master three things. First, they must be able to distinguish letters. They must notice that "j" has a little tail that distinguishes it from "i." (I'll put letters and words in quotation marks when emphasizing what they look like on the page.) Second, they must learn the mapping between these visual symbols and their auditory counterparts—for example, that the letter "o" sometimes goes with one sound (as in the word TONE) but at other times goes with another sound (as in TON). (I'll put letters and words in small capital letters when emphasizing their sound.)

There's a third thing to be learned, and this is the least intuitive for us to appreciate; learning the mapping is not quite what you think. We think that the sound that goes with "t" is TEE, but that's actually *two* sounds, a consonant and vowel sound. Children must be able to hear that TEE is two sounds; they must be able to hear individual speech sounds. To read, children must be able to know what T sounds like *in isolation*, because that's the sound that goes with the letter "t." That turns out to be especially hard for kids. Let's start with the easier tasks and work our way to this tougher one.

The Visual Task in Learning to Read

Most kids find distinguishing one letter from another relatively easy. Sure, some letters are confusable because they have similar shapes (e.g., B, D, P, R) or are the mirror image of another letter (e.g., M/W, b/d). And beginning readers do indeed mix up letters that look similar, a phenomenon also observed in languages other than English. But we shouldn't think this problem is worse than it is. The fortunate fact is that there aren't that many letters to learn, so with some practice, kids get it (figure 1.1).

Learning Letter-to-Sound Mappings

Learning which sound goes with which letter seems rather obviously more challenging. As I noted, some letters do double-duty for sounds: "o" represents one sound in ton and another in tone. There are actually forty-four speech sounds used in English, so such doubling up is inevitable given that we have twenty-six letters. Worse yet, it's not just that two

Figure 1.1. Confusable letters. Even experienced readers occasionally mistake one letter for another, a problem that can be made more likely by unusual fonts. Overall, however, distinguishing one letter from another is not the most common obstacle to learning to decode.
Source: © Jason Covich.

sounds go with a single letter. Sometimes a single sound goes with either of two letters. For example "y" in the middle of words often sounds like "i" as in RHYME.

If you were creating an alphabet for English from scratch, it would be sensible to create forty-four letters and match each speech sound with one letter. But written English, alas, was not created from scratch. Our language is a mongrel: Germanic origins, heavily influenced by Scandinavian (Norman) and French invasions, and later by the adoption of Latinate and Greek words. That's a problem because when we borrowed words, we frequently retained the spelling conventions of the original language.

In consequence, our letter-to-sound mapping is messy. That has caused misery among generations of school children, although it has provided fodder for light rhymers:

When the English tongue we
 speak.
Why is break not rhymed with
 freak?
Will you tell me why it's true
We say sew but likewise few?
And the maker of the verse,
Cannot rhyme his horse with
 worse?
Beard is not the same as
 heard
Cord is different from word.
Cow is cow but low is low
Shoe is never rhymed with foe.
Think of hose, dose, and lose

And think of goose and yet
 with choose
Think of comb, tomb and
 bomb,
Doll and roll or home and some.
Since pay is rhymed with say
Why not paid with said I pray?
Think of blood, food and good.
Mould is not pronounced like
 could.
Wherefore done, but gone and
 lone—
Is there any reason known?
To sum up all, it seems to me
Sound and letters don't agree

And yet things are not as bad as you might first think. English pronunciation looks more consistent when we take context into account. A well-known example of the anything-goes character of English spelling is the invented word "ghoti," to be pronounced FISH—provided one pronounces GH as in the word "enough," O as in the word "women," and TI as in the word "motion." Cute, but there's a reason most would pronounce "ghoti" as GOATEE. The context of each letter matters. When "gh" appears at the start of a word, it's pronounced as a hard g (e.g., GHASTLY, GHOST). In the middle of a word, it's silent (e.g., DAUGHTER, TAUGHT). It's pronounced as F only at the end of a word (LAUGH, TOUGH).

In fact, researchers have found that consonants at the start or end of single-syllable words are pronounced consistently about 90 percent of the time. Vowels in the middle of single-syllable words are pronounced consistently only 60 percent of the time, but when the vowel is an exception, the final consonant frequently helps to determine the pronunciation. So, for example, the vowel string "oo" is usually pronounced as in the word BOOT, but sometimes it's pronounced as in the word BOOK. It turns out that "oo" has the latter pronunciation only when it's followed by "k" or "r" (BOOK, BROOK, CROOK, SHOOK, POOR, DOOR, FLOOR).

There's another reason to take heart about the seemingly crazy pronunciation of English words. Many words that break pronunciation rules are very common. "Gone," "give," are," "were," and "done" all break a rule: *when a word ends with "e," the vowel sound is long.* (Hence, "give" should rhyme with HIVE.) Although these words break the rule, they appear so commonly they are good candidates simply to be memorized as exceptions.

So there's no doubt that learning the mapping between letters and sounds is a challenge, but that's not the aspect of learning to read that most often gives kids trouble. The sticking point is the hearing of the speech sounds. Let's look at why that's so hard.

Learning to Hear Speech Sounds

What sound do you associate with the letter "p"? You might think of it as PUH—that's what parents often tell children—but that's *two* sounds: the sound of the letter "p" and then a vowel sound after it, UH. The sound associated with the letter "p" is actually just a plosion of air—your vocal chords don't vibrate at all. In fact, that's the same plosion of air you make for the letter "b." The only difference is that when you say BEE, your vocal chords vibrate to make the vowel sound *at the same time* you make the plosion of air, whereas when you say PEE, the vocal chords start to vibrate only about .04 seconds *after* the plosion. Yup. The difference between "p" and "b" hinges on this .04 second difference. So asking, "What sound does the letter 'p' make?" is nonsensical. The very definition of the sound depends on its relationship to neighboring sounds. It's actually impossible to say P in isolation.

This problem—the difficulty of isolating speech sounds—is even worse than that. Individual speech sounds also vary depending on the surrounding context. Try this. Put your hand in front of your mouth and say POT. You feel the puff of air when you say the P. Now do the same thing saying SPOT. The puff is stronger for POT than SPOT. So we talk about "the sound the letter 'p' makes" as if there is one sound associated with "p," but that's an abstraction, an ideal.

We're not done yet. Understanding where one word ends and another begins is important for reading—you need to know which sounds are supposed to clump together to form a word. But kids don't hear individual words as well as adults do. In a standard test of this ability, you give the child a short sentence to keep in mind—say, "I like yellow bananas." You give him a small basket of blocks and ask him to arrange a line of them, one block for each word in the sentence. There's no guarantee that the child will pick four blocks for the sentence. It might be three, or five, or seven. He is just not sure where words begin and end (figure 1.2).

Children's ability to hear individual speech sounds can be tested in different ways. They might be asked to name the sound at the beginning of a word. They might be asked if two words begin with the same sound or end with the same sound. In more challenging tasks, they might be asked to change a word by adding, removing, or manipulating sounds, for example, "If I took the word TOP and added a ssss at the beginning, what word would it make?"

If reading is a code between written symbols and speech sounds, it's going to be hard to learn the code if you can't hear those sounds. Lots of research indicates that this reasonable supposition is right. Children who

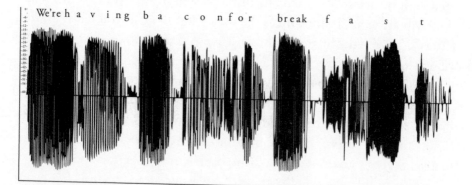

Figure 1.2. Visual representation of a sentence. The author is saying, "We're having bacon for breakfast." Time moves left to right, and the vertical axis shows sound intensity. When people speak, there are not clean breaks between each word, which is probably why children have trouble knowing where words begin and end.
Source: © Daniel Willingham.

have trouble learning to read often have difficulty hearing individual speech sounds. At the other end of the spectrum, children who more or less teach themselves to read turn out to hear them easily. This relationship between the ability to hear speech sounds and reading is not unique to learning to read English—you see it across languages.

So we have our first clue about how we can help kids become good readers: help them with this auditory challenge.

THE ROLE OF KNOWLEDGE IN COMPREHENSION

So far, I have discussed decoding and reading as though they were synonyms, but obviously there's more to reading than sounding out words. A child might read aloud, "the farmer in the dell," and perhaps recognize the phrase from the song, but if he doesn't know that a dell is a small valley, he's not fully understanding the meaning of what he's read. It's equally obvious that in order to understand, a reader must use syntactic rules that relate words to one another. Syntactic rules determine the difference in meaning between, "Dan wished he had sung better," and, "He wished Dan had sung better"—same words, slightly different order, quite different meanings.

We'll skip discussing the mental processes that allow us to understand the meaning of individual words like "farmer" and "in," as well as the mental processes that assign syntactic roles to individual words so that they are connected into a sentence. Fascinating as these processes are, they usually pose few problems to young readers, or when they do, it's for easily appreciated reasons. For example, a reader won't understand a text that uses unfamiliar vocabulary ("This class needs realia") or syntax so complex it's hard to unravel (e.g. "The dog that the man whom the cat saw kicked yelped"). When the former happens, you look the word up. When the latter happens, you complain of poor writing.

Building Meaning across Sentences

Processes of reading comprehension that go beyond the individual word and sentence are less obvious. There must be some way that we can make meaning across sentences—something akin to the way syntax connects meaning across words. For example, consider these two sentences: "The octogenarian scientist approached the podium to collect his Nobel prize, head down, embarrassed by the applause. He chuckled softly to himself." To understand this brief text, we must recognize that "he" in the second sentence and "the octogenarian scientist" from the first sentence refer to the same person. We must also understand that the chuckling in the second sentence is directly related to the information provided in the first sentence; the information explains *why* he was chuckling. How do we connect ideas from the sentence we're currently reading to something we read earlier?

The answer rests on a distinction between given and new information. Given information is stuff that you have already been told in the text. New information is stuff you haven't. Most writing alternates between the two: you are reminded of something you were already told, and then you're told something new. Then something old again, then something new.

For example, suppose you read, "Some beer is in the car trunk. The beer is warm." In the second sentence, the reference to "the beer" is the given information. The given information directs your attention to an idea from an earlier sentence. *Ah*, you think, *we're talking about the beer again.* Once you've focused on that idea, the new information in the sentence provides something to add, and you connect it to the given information. So you will connect "warm" in the second sentence to "the beer" from the first sentence (figure 1.3).

This given-new principle is powerful enough that it's jarring to read prose that violates it. For example, suppose you read: "Some beer is in the car

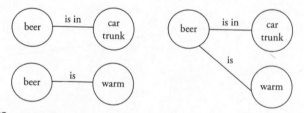

Figure 1.3. How sentences are connected. At left is a cartoon version of the formal way that a psychologist would diagram your understanding of the two sentences in the text. When you read "the beer is warm," you look for some overlap between this sentence and the ideas in the one you had already read. When you find the overlap (the reference to "beer"), that tells you it's a way to connect the two sentences. The connection is shown at right.

Source: © Daniel Willingham.

trunk. The beer is warm. The beer is not cold." The third sentence has given information (the beer) that doesn't add anything new; if you know it's warm, obviously it's not cold. That's so odd that you might struggle to find a way to interpret the third sentence so that it *does* tell you something new. (Perhaps the repetition is meant to signal that the beer was supposed to be cold.) Likewise, it sounds very strange to read a sentence that doesn't mention any given information, as in this example: "Some beer is in the car trunk. Deciduous trees lose their leaves in the fall." You have no way to connect the second sentence to what you've read so far. That's what makes it a non sequitur.

This type of connection is important but pretty limited. I tell you something about beer; then I tell you another fact about the beer. That's fine as far as it goes; sometimes I want to tell you several things about beer (or whatever else), so the beer is the given, and I keep telling you new things about it.

More common, however, are causal connections. For example, consider these two sentences: "Trisha spilled her coffee. Dan jumped from his chair to get a rag." I'm sure the second sentence did not feel like a non sequitur to you; you easily connected them. But wait a minute. If connections happen when there is given and new information, where is the "given" information in the second sentence? Where did I repeat something I already told you?

The given information is not really in the text. It's in your head. You inferred it. You know that spilled coffee makes a mess. You know that when a mess is made, people usually clean it, and often do so immediately. You know that rags are often used to clean messes.

Now the writer could have included all of this information in the text. He could have written, "Trisha spilled her coffee. The coffee made a mess on the floor. Dan wanted to clean the mess. Dan had rags in the kitchen that he used for cleaning. Dan jumped from his chair to get a rag." In this version, the given information is made explicit, but the reason that writers (and speakers) omit information is plain: if you didn't omit stuff that the reader knows anyway, simple communication would be terribly boring.

The author can't include every last bit of information that's needed to make her writing comprehensible lest she tell the reader things he already knows. But then again, every time she elects to leave out some information, she's gambling. She's assuming that the reader has the omitted information in memory. What if the writer is wrong? Then the reader will not be able to connect the sentences and comprehension will fail. That's what happens when you start to read an article on some unfamiliar technical subject: it's written for an audience with a lot of knowledge you lack.

But comprehension doesn't always fail. Sometimes you can deduce the missing information from the context. Reading researcher Walter Kintsch offered this example: "Connors used Kevlar sails because he expected little wind." All I know about Kevlar is that it's some sort of fabric. I sure didn't know that it is used for sails, but that's easy to infer from the context, right? So what's the problem with reading this sentence? (See figure 1.4.) No

Figure 1.4. Context resolves ambiguity. This sign assumes a certain amount of background knowledge that is left unstated. For what are you to check your zipper? Should I check all zippers on my person, even the zipper on my briefcase? The ambiguity is resolved by the context: this sign appeared on the exit door of a men's bathroom. *Source:* © Daniel Willingham.

problem. In fact, that's one of the great pleasures of reading. You learn new things, for example, that sails can be made of Kevlar. But figuring things out in this way amounts to problem solving and solving problems takes time and mental effort. It's not just that you have to think about what "Kevlar" might mean; it's also that figuring that out interrupts the flow of the text in which you find it. You may lose the thread of the argument or story. A bit of this sort of problem solving is satisfying, even fun. Too much of it makes reading slow and difficult.

Just how much unknown stuff can a text have in it before a reader will declare, "Mental overload!" and call it quits? That surely varies depending on the reader's attitude toward reading and motivation to understand that particular text. Still, studies have measured readers' tolerance of unfamiliar vocabulary and have estimated that readers need to know about 98 percent of the words for comfortable comprehension. That may sound high, but bear in mind that the paragraph you're reading now has about seventy-five unique words. So 98 percent familiarity means that this and every other paragraph like it would have one or two words you don't know. That's a lot.

What's a "Good Reader"?

The discussion to this point implies that people who are good readers are people who know a lot. A lot of what? What kind of knowledge makes you a good reader? That depends on what you want to read. Authors omit information based on their guess as to what their audience already knows. A writer for the *Journal of the Lepidopterist's Society* will omit a whole lot of information about butterflies, figuring that her audience already knows it.

Most parents want their children to be solid *general* readers. They aren't worried about their kids reading professional journals for butterfly collectors, but they expect their kids to be able to read the *New York Times, National Geographic,* or other materials written for the thoughtful layperson. A writer for the *New York Times* will not assume deep knowledge about postage stamps, or African geography, or Elizabethan playwrights—but she will assume some knowledge about each. To be a good general reader, your child needs knowledge of the world that's a million miles wide and an inch deep—wide enough to recognize the titles *The Jew of Malta* and *The*

Merchant of Venice, for example, but not that the former may have inspired the latter. Enough to know that rare stamps can be very valuable, but not the going price of the rare Inverted Jenny stamp of 1918.

If being a "good reader" actually means "knowing a little bit about a lot of stuff," then reading tests don't work quite the way most people think they do. Reading tests purport to measure a student's ability to read, and "ability to read" sounds like a general skill. Once I know your ability to read, I ought to be able (roughly) to predict your comprehension of any text I hand you. But I've just said that reading comprehension depends heavily on how much you happen to know about the topic of the text, because that determines your ability to make up for the information the writer felt free to omit. Perhaps, then, reading comprehension tests are really knowledge tests in disguise.

There is reason to think that's true. In one study, researchers measured the reading ability of eleventh graders with a standard reading test and also administered tests of what they called "cultural literacy"—students' knowledge of mainstream culture. There were tests of the names of artists, entertainers, military leaders, musicians, philosophers, and scientists, as well as separate tests of factual knowledge of science, history, and literature. The researchers found robust correlations between scores on the reading test and scores on the various cultural literacy tests—correlations between 0.55 and 0.90.*

So Where Do You Get Broad Knowledge?

If knowledge is so important to reading, where do you get it? Many sources, of course: conversations, television, movies, the Internet. But research has shown that people with broad general knowledge—the type of knowledge that makes good general readers—gained most of that

---

*A correlation is a way of measuring whether two variables are related. A correlation of 0.0 means there is no relationship at all, as we might expect between, say, people's shoe size and how much they like ice cream. A correlation of 1.0 means a perfect relationship—for example, the height of people measured in inches and the height measured in centimeters. To give some perspective on what a correlation of 0.60 means, that's about the correlation of the average height of parents and the average height of their children.

knowledge by reading. (This work was conducted before access to the Internet was widespread, but in Chapter 9, I discuss other research indicating that kids aren't likely to gain much knowledge from most of their online activities.)

Here's how researchers tested this hypothesis. First, they needed a measure of how much people had read when they were growing up. They could have asked, "Were you a reader as a kid?" but that's a pretty subjective judgment. Researchers figured that readers would be more likely to recognize the names of well-known authors, books, and magazines, so they gave people a list of author names and titles; some were real, and some they had made up to sound plausible. (Exhibit 1.1 shows a sample of magazine titles.) Subjects were asked to identify the real ones.

Exhibit 1.1.
Recognition Test of Magazine Titles

Can you pick out the genuine magazine titles from the false ones? Answers are at the end of the chapter.

Architecture Today	*Madame*
Better Homes and Gardens	*New Republic*
Car and Driver	*Scientific American*
Digital Sound	*Technology Digest*
Home and Yard	*Town and Country*

Their prediction was that people who did well on this test must have done a lot of reading, and so scores on the test would be positively correlated with knowing a lot of stuff. To get a measure of "knowing a lot of stuff," they used a battery of tests measuring common knowledge of science, history, the arts, and so on.

The results did show a substantial correlation; people who recognized a lot of author and magazine names had very broad cultural knowledge. But of course that relationship could be due to something else—it's correlation, not causation. The most obvious candidate would be intelligence.

Maybe smart people like to read as kids and smart people know a lot. So the researchers used another battery of measures to get at intelligence— metrics like high school grade point average and performance on a standard intelligence test. And indeed, intelligence was related to how much college students knew. Related, but not the whole story. Reading volume was still a big contributor. In other words, smart people (high IQ, good grades) who never read much as kids didn't have a lot of general knowledge as adults. And not-so-smart people (low IQ, poor grades) who read a lot as kids did have a lot of general knowledge.

So we've come full circle. We began by examining how sentences are connected to build larger meanings and quickly came to the idea that the reader must bring knowledge to this process to make up for the information that the writer omitted. We noted that sometimes the reader who lacks this knowledge can use the rest of the text and some reasoning power to make up for this missing knowledge; that's what happened when I learned that sails can be made of Kevlar. Finally, we saw that this process is not only possible, but seems to be very important to reading, because adults with broad background knowledge (which helps them to be good readers) got that background knowledge by reading. You need knowledge to read, and reading gives you knowledge.

So now we have our second clue about how to help children become good readers. They need a broad foundation of knowledge of words and the world.

MOTIVATION

A boy might be motivated to read *Looking for Alaska* to impress a girl or because it was assigned in school. It seems self-evident that these are not the sort of motivators we're after because they're temporary. We want our kids to read because they have a positive attitude toward reading, because they find the activity itself rewarding. Unfortunately, although kids like reading (both at home and at school) in the early grades, their opinions become more and more negative as they get older. By high school, the average kid is at best indifferent to reading. What can be done to change that?

Attitudes toward Reading

Before thinking about how to change reading mind-sets, we need to know what type of attitude we're dealing with. Some attitudes are the product of a logical analysis, at least, as logical as we can make them. I recently bought a dishwasher, and my attitudes toward dishwasher brands (I like Kenmore, I don't like Whirlpool, and I think Bosch is overrated) are a product of research on repair records, efficiency, and so on. My opinions are pretty cold and pretty rational.

We like to think that most of our attitudes are rational, that our opinions are the product of fact gathering and logical analysis. But we have attitudes about things where analysis is impossible, or at least much less likely. Why do you prefer Coke to Pepsi, or Old Spice to Brut? No one says, "I've looked into the matter, and research shows that Old Spice makes a man more attractive to women and tends to make other men submissive." You use Old Spice because you like the way it smells, and, perhaps equally important, you like the way it makes you *feel*. These are emotional attitudes. Emotions also play heavily in attitudes to things that are intertwined with our values—issues like abortion or capital punishment. You could bring logical analysis to bear on such issues, and people like to think that they do. But the logical arguments are mostly post hoc and marshaled to justify the emotionally driven opinion.

It's a good bet—although there's limited research on this question— that a child's reading attitude is mostly emotional. It's not a reasoned judgment of its value to her future career prospects. It's based on whether reading seems rewarding, excites her, interests her. So where do emotional attitudes come from?

The Origins of Emotional Attitudes

Here's Oprah Winfrey on reading: "Books were my pass to personal freedom. I learned to read at age three, and discovered there was a whole world to conquer that went beyond our farm in Mississippi." One source—probably the primary source—of positive reading attitudes is positive reading experiences. This phenomenon is no more complicated than understanding why someone has a positive attitude toward eggplant: you taste it and

Figure 1.5. Twentieth-century writer Richard Wright. In his autobiography, Wright describes his first encounter with a fictional story. A young woman—a teacher who boarded at Wright's grandmother's house—learned that he was unfamiliar with children's stories and so told him a pirate's tale. He was bewitched: "My sense of life deepened, and the feel of things was different, somehow. The sensations the story aroused in me were never to leave me."
Source: Carl Van Vechten photograph, retrieved from http://www.loc.gov/pictures/item/2004663766/

like it. Oprah tasted the mental journeys reading affords and loved them (figure 1.5).

We can elaborate a bit on this obvious relationship. Kids who like to read also tend to be strong readers as measured by standard reading tests. Again, this is not terribly surprising: we usually like what we're good at, and vice versa. This situation yields a positive feedback loop (figure 1.6).

If you're a good reader, you're more likely to enjoy a story because reading it doesn't seem like work. That enjoyment means that you have a better attitude toward reading; that is, you believe that reading is a pleasurable, valuable thing to do. A better attitude means you read more often, and more reading makes you even better at reading: your decoding gets better and better, and all that reading you're doing adds to your background knowledge. We would also predict the inverse to be true: if reading is difficult, you won't enjoy it; you'll have a negative attitude toward the activity, and you'll avoid it when possible, meaning that you'll fall still

Figure 1.6. Reading virtuous cycle.
Source: © Daniel Willingham.

further behind your peers. This cycle has been called "the Matthew effect" from the biblical verse, "For whosoever hath, to him shall be given, and he shall have more abundance; but whosoever hath not, from him shall be taken away even that he hath" (Matthew, 25:29). More succinctly, the rich get richer and the poor get poorer.

Reading Self-Concept

As you probably know, Twitter is a website that allows users to broadcast very short messages. Users are also invited to compose a brief profile—a self-description that anyone can view. The profile is limited to 160 characters, so users must be concise; to give you a sense of the need for brevity, the sentence you're now reading is forty-nine characters too long. If you don't have a Twitter account, consider for a moment how you might describe yourself in 160 characters. For economy, many people write a series of self-descriptive phrases (figure 1.7). Twitter profiles are not a bad way of thinking about our self-concept. It's a cluster of generalizations about how we tend to act (introvert, activist) and roles we fill (professor, father).

Here we're interested in one narrow aspect of the self: how you see yourself when it comes to reading. Your reading self-concept is probably related to your attitude toward reading, but the two are not synonymous. You might think that reading is useful (and so your attitude is positive) and also see yourself as quite competent as a reader. But you don't see it as an important part of who you are. For that reason, I think that reading self-concept is more important than reading attitudes. The purpose of this book is not to help you raise a child who has a positive attitude toward reading but never reads.

1. Spreading love with every invention, forever devoted to the kingdom of monsters.	A. Alicia Keys
2. Passionate about my work, in love with my family and dedicated to spreading light.	B. Ashton Kutcher
3. I make stuff, actually I make up stuff, stories mostly, collaborations of thoughts, dreams, and actions. Thats me.	C. Lady Gaga
4. Astrophysicist	D. Jimmy Fallon

Figure 1.7. Twitter bios as statements of self-concept. When we're forced to be concise, our self-descriptions often refer to roles we play and personality descriptions. See if you can match the Twitter biography (left) with the writer (right).
Source: Twitter profile text obtained from Twitter.com, September 8, 2014.

If "reader" is part of your self-concept, it will occur to you as a viable activity more often. "What will I do on that two-hour train trip? I could bring my iPod. Oh, I should bring a book too." And of course, the more you read, the more "reader" becomes cemented as part of your self-concept. What I do and what I think of myself reinforce one another (figure 1.8). Conversely, children who do not have "reader" as part of their self-concept are not likely to think of it as an option. They may be neutral or even mildly positive in their attitudes toward reading but do not see it as "one of the things I do." Analogously, I don't make a conscious decision not to attend renaissance fairs. It's not that I don't like them. It never even occurs to me to think about whether I might enjoy going (figure 1.8).

Why does one four-year-old have a developing sense of herself as a reader and another not? It seems obvious that I would think of myself as a reader if I read a lot. That's true, and it's especially true if I perceive that I read more than other people do; it's something that separates me from my peers. Very young children don't engage in such extensive comparisons; that's

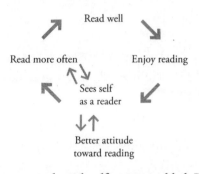

Figure 1.8. Reading virtuous cycle with self-concept added. Reading self-concept is both built by and a contributor to positive reading attitudes and the act of reading. *Source:* © Daniel Willingham.

for older kids. Still, you want your child to read at an early age (even if "reading" means looking at pictures) in order to build a reading self-concept.

Looking over this section on reading motivation, it may seem that we've made little progress. I identified two important factors: positive reading attitudes and a sense of oneself as a reader. But the genesis of each is predicated on your child's doing some reading, and that's the problem we're trying to solve. If your child were doing a lot of reading, we wouldn't be concerned about his attitude or self-concept. That conundrum harkens back to our discussion of reading comprehension in which I said that the way to improve reading comprehension is to improve the child's background knowledge, and the way to improve background knowledge is to read. So the secret to raising kids who read is to have reading kids?

In part, yes. And maybe it shouldn't be surprising that reading is the best way to support good decoding, comprehension, and motivation. Still, we need a way out of that revolving door, and in the chapters that follow I'll suggest two tactics. First, we examine ways other than reading that support decoding, comprehension, and motivation. Second, we look at ways to get your child reading even if his attitudes are not that positive and his reading self-concept is weak. The hope is that kick-starting reading will generate a positive feedback cycle.

Let's get started.

Answers to exhibit 1.1: The actual titles are: *Better Homes and Gardens, Car and Driver, New Republic, Scientific American,* and *Town and Country.*

Notes

"a phenomenon also observed in languages other than English": Treiman and Kessler (2003); Treiman, Kessler, and Pollo (2006); Treiman, Levin, and Kessler (2012).

"light rhymers": Vaughn (1902).

"Many words that break pronunciation rules are very common.": Ziegler, Stone, and Jacobs (1997).

"just not sure where words begin and end": Holden and MacGinitie (1972).

"Children who have trouble learning to read often have difficulty hearing individual speech sounds.": Melby-Lervåg, Lyster, and Hulme (2012).

"children who more or less teach themselves to read turn out to hear them easily": Backman (1983).

"you see it across languages": Anthony and Francis (2005); Hu and Catts (1998).

"Kintsch offered this example": Kintsch (2012).

"Too much of it makes reading slow and difficult.": Foertsch and Gernsbacher (1994).

"readers need to know about 98 percent of the words": Carver (1994); Schmitt, Jiang, and Grabe (2011).

"The researchers found robust correlations between scores on the reading test and scores on the various cultural literacy tests.": Cunningham and Stanovich (1991, 1997); Stanovich and Cunningham (1993); Stanovich, Cunningham, and West (1995); see also Anderson, Wilson, and Fielding (1988).

"their opinions become more and more negative as they get older": Eccles, Wigfield, Harold, Blumenfeld, and Url (1993); Jacobs, Lanza, Osgood, Eccles, and Wigfield (2002); Kush and Watkins (1996); McKenna, Conradi, and Meyer (2012); McKenna, Kear, and Ellsworth (1995).

"we have attitudes about things where analysis is impossible": For a review of the three types of attitudes, see Aronson, Wilson, and Akert (2012).

"the logical arguments are mostly post hoc and marshaled to justify the emotional opinion": For a review of this literature, see Haidt (2012).

"This situation yields a positive feedback loop.": Mol and Bus (2011).

"your decoding gets better and better, and all that reading you're doing adds to your background knowledge": The best evidence for this assertion comes from studies that employ structural equation models (e.g., Clark & DeZoysa, 2011). For data that examine the relationship across countries, see Lee (2014).

"The Matthew effect": Stanovich (1986).

"the rich get richer and the poor get poorer": Morgan and Fuchs (2007).

"if 'reader' is part of your self-concept": For more on reading self-identity, see Hall (2012).

"What I do and what I think of myself reinforce one another": Retelsdorf, Köller, and Möller (2014).

PART I

BIRTH THROUGH PRESCHOOL

2

PREPARING YOUR CHILD TO LEARN TO DECODE

You may have seen products like the video series Your Baby Can Read! that purport to teach reading skills to children as young as three months old. Actually, your baby can't read, with or without such videos, but there are things you can do that will smooth the way once reading instruction begins years later.

HELPING YOUR CHILD HEAR SPEECH SOUNDS

In chapter 1, I emphasized the importance of hearing individual speech sounds. Children who come to school with that skill in place have a real edge in learning to read compared to those who don't. But this skill doesn't develop spontaneously. Syllables are much easier to hear than individual speech sounds. Adults who cannot read can probably tell you that CARROT and DOGGY have more syllables than SAT. But illiterate adults cannot tell you that CARROT and SAT end with the same sound, which differs from the one at the end of DOGGY. How can you help your child hear speech sounds before she can read?

Motherese

The evidence for the first method is not terribly strong, but it points to something you would probably do anyway, so I'll mention it. You may well have heard about the scientific study of "motherese," the somewhat precious name given to the way mothers speak to their infant children.

"I <u>do</u> realise this probably indicates a certain lack
of fundamental maturity but I actually prefer baby talk."

Figure 2.1. Motherese. Speaking to children in motherese helps children learn to speak and is not talking down to children. But there does come a time that the child is ready for adult speech.
Source: © Mike Williams, via CartoonStock.

Compared to adult speech, motherese is spoken more slowly and at a higher pitch. The grammar is simpler, and the prosody is exaggerated. (Prosody is the sort of melody of speech, including features like tone and pacing. For example, in English, a rising pitch at the end of a sentence signals a question.)

Parents speaking motherese probably help their children learn to talk by providing a very clear model of speech. And perhaps because of its slow pace and clarity of enunciation, motherese may give children an advantage in hearing speech sounds years later (figure 2.1).

Wordplay

The evidence is much stronger for the second method: wordplay that highlights individual speech sounds. In some instances, the child listens to others engaged in such play; those activities can begin as early in life as you care to start. Other games require that your child produces some wordplay on her own. You'll probably want to start those at age four or five, or earlier, if your child catches on to the idea. Here are some examples of word games that help children to hear individual speech sounds:

- **Some children's songs and rhymes center on word play,** for example, The Name Game ("Dan, Dan, bo-Ban, banana-fana fo-Fan, fee fi-mo-Man. Dan!") and Apples and Bananas ("I like to eat, eat, eat, eeples and baneenees").
- **Classic nursery rhymes** use much of this sort of word play. So do Dr. Seuss, Shel Silverstein, and other children's authors.
- **Sing songs they know, replacing the initial letter of each word with the letter of your choice,** for example, "Mary had a little lamb" becomes "Bary bad a bittle bamb."
- **Find excuses for alliteration:** "Great golly! Gobs of grapes!"
- **Spoonerisms are comic gold for kids this age:** "mighty fish" becomes "fighty mish," for example.
- This one is tricky: **take the first letter of the month you were born and replace the first letter (or blend) of your name:** "February" + "Mike" becomes "Fike." For the rest of the day, your name is Fike.
- **Compound words** are fascinating for kids. "It's called a scarecrow because it scares crows." So are homonyms and homophones like "I" and "eye."

These sorts of word games do more than help kids hear speech sounds. They also show your children that you're interested in language: you find it fun and worthy of close attention.

Don't get frantic about ensuring enough "practice" with these games. There's lots of research on classroom instructional programs that have kids practice tasks that boost awareness of speech sounds. The exercises tend to be straightforward questions like asking, "Do 'can' and 'man' rhyme?" or, "Can you squish together 'ssss,' 'aaaa,' and 'tuh' and tell me what word it makes?" Researchers estimate that for most children, a total of twenty or twenty-five hours of such tasks (with feedback) is sufficient.

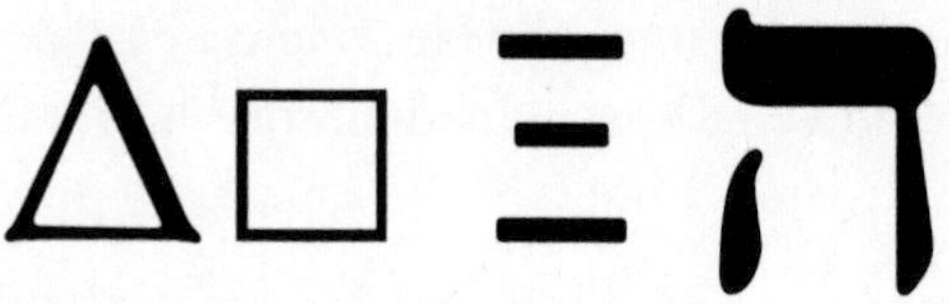

Figure 2.2. Distinctive letters. Letters could be closed figures made of straight line segments (like the two at the left) or they could include line segments that do not touch (like the two at the right). Our Roman alphabet includes neither sort. *Source:* © Daniel Willingham.

LEARNING LETTERS

As long as you're working on sounds, should you also teach your four-year-old the letters of the alphabet? It *seems* as if learning the alphabet would probably be hard for children, so maybe it would be good to start early. It seems hard simply because, as noted in chapter 1, letters look so confusable. When you think about it, it seems odd that they aren't more distinct (figure 2.2).

Still, although letters look confusable and kids do mix them up, most kids get it with some practice. But is there any advantage to learning letters before reading instruction begins in kindergarten?

Teaching Letter Names

The research on this question is not completely straightforward. On the one hand, the kids who come to kindergarten knowing their letters are the ones who end up being better readers later, and that finding has been known for decades. On the other hand, teaching kids their letters early doesn't seem to give them much of an edge in reading. Why? The obvious answer would be that knowing letters doesn't actually help; letter knowledge and reading success are associated because knowing the letters happens to go along with some other knowledge that is helping kids with reading. One possibility is that kids get a head start on knowing the letter-sound associations through letter names. No one really knows, but it seems to me that learning letters at home shouldn't be something you overworry about.

Print Referencing

If you still like the idea of your child learning letters, there are ways other than explicit instruction that you can make that happen. The one with the best research base is *print referencing*, a way of reading a book aloud to your child. In typical read-alouds, kids gain very little knowledge about letters. They don't learn letter names, or the sounds they are associated with, or what letters look like. Why? Because even if the words are visible, eye-tracking studies show that kids don't look at letters during read-alouds. They look at pictures.

In print referencing, the adult draws the child's attention to print. Some techniques are explicit. You might make a request (e.g., "Can you show me where on the page I should start reading?") or a comment (e.g., "Look; these two words are exactly the same"). The adult also draws the child's attention to print implicitly by pointing to the words as he reads them.

There is good evidence that children learn about print when they are read to this way. I believe the data—I think print referencing works—but I'm nevertheless not a big fan of print referencing. Whether you're a toddler or an adult, you can't think of different things at the same time. If you're thinking about letters, you're not following the story. I'd rather the child thought about the story. Obviously, if it's an alphabet book, the letters *are* the story. And my general orientation will always be trumped by the child's interest: if he shows any interest in the print, by all means talk about the print.

Letters in the Wild

Rather than talk about letters during reading time, I'd rather talk about letters when we can focus on the idea of letters alone. Your child is surrounded by print: on stop signs, cereal boxes, and familiar logos like Disney or Lego (figure 2.3).

How can you get started in exploiting all the print in your child's world? The foundational idea is that you can gain information from print: Mommy knows where to get off the highway because the green signs with the white shapes tell her where things are. How does Daddy know this cereal has a lot of sugar in it? He read the box. Next, your child might come to see that it's the *letters* that carry meaning. They have nonarbitrary shapes and are arranged in a particular order. Your child might deduce these facts on his own, but there's no reason not to point them out when you're stuck in line at Costco and he remarks on the sign.

Once your child gets the basic idea—reading carries meaning, and does so through letters—there is no end to the games you can play. I mean sure,

Figure 2.3. Letters and logos. Telling your child about the letters in logos like the "M" in McDonald's is an easy way to make her aware that she's surrounded by print. *Source:* © Mike Mozart via Flickr.

get them blocks with letters on them, get them letter refrigerator magnets, get them alphabet board books . . . but also be opportunistic about times and places that letters can sneak into your child's day. Make letters in the mud with a stick when you take a breather on a hike. Draw the Batman logo *and* a "B" in the steam on the bathroom mirror. Make everyone a pancake in the shape of his or her first initial. Stopped at a red light: "Let's see how many 't's we can see on the signs around here before the light turns green." If you prompt interest in letters in these daily interactions, it's that much more likely your child will show interest in letters during read-alouds.

WHEN SHOULD READING INSTRUCTION START?

As with learning letters, there are some twists and turns in the research on this question. I said in chapter 1 that there is more consistency in the mapping between letters and sounds than is first apparent. But that doesn't mean that all of those rules are easy to learn. Yes, we can make sense of the fact that "c" is sometimes pronounced s and sometimes κ: it's the former when it's followed by "e," "i," or "y" (e.g., CENT, CINCH, or CYCLE) and the latter when followed by other vowels (e.g., CAT, COLLAR, or CULPRIT). But even if there's a rule to explain the inconsistency, learning would be simpler if it were always pronounced the same way.

The complexity of the code in English is a problem for beginning readers that kids learning to read other languages don't face because the letter-sound mapping is simpler. Finnish and Italian, for example, are very consistent, with a near one-to-one mapping between letters and speech sounds. Kids learn to decode quite quickly in those countries. In a matter of months, most children can read aloud one- or two-syllable words with few errors. English-speaking children lag far behind (figure 2.4).

Figure 2.4. Reading proficiency in European countries. The numbers are the average percentages of one-syllable words that children can read correctly at the end of first grade. Portuguese, French, and Danish, like English, have less consistent mappings between sounds and letters than other languages do.

Source: © hektoR, Shutterstock. Modified from the original. Percentages from Seymour, Aro, and Erskine (2003).

Learning to decode is harder in English, so it's natural to say, "Start early!" I don't think there's anything wrong with this idea, but there are some data indicating that starting as early as five years old or as late as seven doesn't end up making much difference. Of course, kids who start earlier will be better readers at age eight, but the difference is pretty much gone by age eleven. Why does the advantage disappear so quickly? Because kids who start earlier learn to decode earlier. But by age eleven, everyone, including the late starters, is a good decoder. For that reason, reading tests for eleven-year-olds also change; there's no point in measuring decoding because everyone is pretty good at it. Instead, reading tests emphasize comprehension, which, we saw in chapter 1, depends heavily on background knowledge. So having learned to decode at a younger age doesn't provide an edge.

Thus, I wouldn't look for a preschool that proudly proclaims that it starts reading instruction at age four in order to give kids a head start. Rather, I'd look for a preschool that is sensitive to where my child is and has the flexibility to adapt. If my child is weak in hearing speech sounds, I'd rather she work on that for a while. Then again, if my child shows interest in learning to read, I'd like the school to support her interest.

When it comes to reading and preschools, I'd be more concerned about opportunities for my child to learn about the world than to learn about the alphabet. By age nine or so, your child will likely be a competent decoder. When that happens, his ability to comprehend what he reads will depend heavily on his background knowledge. The time to begin that learning is not, however, at age nine. The time to begin is infancy. So let's get cracking.

Keeping It Simple Summary

- Play games to help your child hear speech sounds.
- Teach the ideas that print carries meaning and that letters go with sounds.

Notes

"Actually, your baby can't read, with or without such videos": Neuman, Kaefer, Pinkham, and Strouse (2014).

"Parents speaking motherese probably help their children learn to talk": Nelson, Hirsh-Pasek, Jusczyk, and Cassidy (1989).

"motherese may give children an advantage in hearing speech sounds": Silvén, Niemi, and Voeten (2002).

"a total of twenty or twenty-five hours of such tasks (with feedback) is sufficient": National Institute of Child Health and Human Development (2000).

"the kids who come to kindergarten knowing their letters are the ones who end up being better readers later": Chall (1967); Noel Foulin (2005).

"teaching kids their letters early doesn't seem to give them much of an edge in reading": Piasta and Wagner (2010).

"a head start on knowing the letter-sound associations through letter names": Treiman and Kessler (2003).

"typical read-alouds, kids gain very little knowledge about letters": Evans, Shaw, and Bell (2000); Hood, Conlon, and Andrews (2008).

"eye-tracking studies show that kids don't look at letters": Justice, Skibbe, Canning, and Lankford (2005).

"children learn about print when they are read to this way": For a review, see Justice and Pullen (2003).

"Your child is surrounded by print": Neumann, Hood, Ford, and Neumann (2011).

"They have non-arbitrary shapes": Levy, Gong, Hessels, Evans, and Jared (2006).

3

CREATING A THIRST FOR KNOWLEDGE

In chapter 2, we saw that parents can prepare their children for reading instruction by ensuring that kids can hear individual speech sounds. It's noteworthy that this learning takes place over months or even years, and that its impact on reading is invisible to both parents and children. Then, when reading instruction begins, the knowledge suddenly becomes relevant.

The same is true of vocabulary and background knowledge (i.e., general knowledge about the world). You'll recall from chapter 1 that they are prime contributors to comprehension; they're needed to fill information gaps that writers leave. Background knowledge takes a central role rather abruptly as reading shifts from being mostly about decoding from kindergarten through second grade to being mostly about comprehension in third grade and beyond. One consequence is that kids who don't have very rich background knowledge—often those from impoverished homes—start to struggle with reading in third or fourth grade, even though they had been doing fine up to that point. This phenomenon is so often observed that it has a name: the fourth-grade slump.

Obviously, you don't want to address the need for knowledge in fourth grade, when it becomes urgent. Knowledge accretes slowly, and it's best to begin at birth. Let's start with vocabulary.

BUILDING VOCABULARY

In what is becoming a repeating theme, I'll start by observing that things get started earlier than you might guess. Infants learn words well before they can speak. Here's an example of an experiment showing that. Researchers

Figure 3.1. Baby ready to participate in a study that will measure brain activity.
Source: © Cat Thrasher, via CatThrasher.com.

recorded brain activity in nine-month-olds. A little cap, fitted with electrodes, was put on the infant's head. Each electrode recorded, through the skull, the activity of the several million neurons below it (figure 3.1).

Researchers were looking for a particular brain response that happens when we perceive something meaningful. For example, suppose you were watching a screen and saw each of these letter strings appear, one at a time:

yare
pova
book

The third stimulus would prompt a particular brain response because it's a meaningful word. Touch the very top of your head, move your finger an inch or two back, and then find spots to the left and right, about an inch or two down. That's where the response happens, about 0.4 seconds after you see the word "book."

In this experiment a baby sat on her (or his) mom's lap, both of them facing a screen. On each trial, Mom would point out an object, even though one was not visible. For example, she might say, "Look, there's a duck!" Then the screen would drop, and behind it would be either the object she named (a toy duck) or some other object (a brush, for example). Other experiments have shown that the "this means something" brain response is exaggerated when there is a mismatch between meanings. It's as though you hear the word "duck" and then see a hairbrush, so you're combing through the part of the brain that deals with meaning, trying to make sense of what just happened. Infants as young as nine months old show this response, strong evidence that they have already learned the meaning of some words.

This result implies that your baby will be learning vocabulary even though he can't show you that he's learning it. So talk to him. Describe what you're doing as you're making dinner and he's in his high chair. Ask his opinion about whether to buy yellow or white onions when you're in the grocery store, even if the question draws only a solemn look. This talk from you doesn't need to be didactic. It can (and, to my taste, should) be social.

For older children—say, age three and up—there are lots of data showing that children mirror the type of talk that they hear—both talk directed to them and talk that they overhear. I remember being startled when my youngest child, then three, walked up to me and asked, "Daddy, is your lap available?" She had learned the concept of "availability" in reference to materials at her preschool and applied it to my lap, which she required at that moment for sitting.

As always, common sense rules here. I'm not suggesting that you salt your conversation with words you've found on a build-your-vocabulary website. "Gosh, José, you're turning into the house factotum, aren't you, my boy?" I'm suggesting that you pay attention to how you talk to your kids, with an eye toward perhaps talking more as you do to adults. They can probably handle it and would benefit. And I guess I'm also suggesting not to speak motherese once they are no longer babies. (Part of that, I'll admit, is personal. It makes my skin crawl to hear a parent in a restaurant use an overly loud, fake-joyous voice to shout in the face of a six-year-old, "Does Biwwy want some owange zuice?").

BUILDING KNOWLEDGE

Between the ages of two and five, your child is a terrific ally in the pursuit of knowledge because that's when she's constantly asking you questions. Sure, not all questions from kids are meant to learn things. Sometimes they want your attention ("Mommy?") and sometimes they make a request ("Can you please open the window?") or ask for permission ("Can I play Nintendo?"). But about two-thirds of the questions that kids around this age pose are meant to elicit information. They want to learn about their world. You can see their desire in the pattern of questions they ask. About half of them are sequenced; they ask for an explanation of something, for example, and the answer prompts a new question as the child digs deeper. And if the answer doesn't provide the requested information, the child will ask again.

So the obvious starting point in helping your child to build knowledge is to answer his questions. You are close at hand and know so much. Even better, you're providing information that he's shown you he's curious about. Not only does your child actually get the answer to his question, but it gives you the chance to communicate to him that questions are valued in your family (figure 3.2).

Figure 3.2. Eleanor Roosevelt on curiosity. "I think, at a child's birth, if a mother could ask a fairy godmother to endow it with the most useful gift, that gift should be curiosity." In fact every child *does* have that gift, but it starts to wither in most around age seven. The question for parents is how to ensure a sturdy curiosity throughout childhood. The answer is showing that you value curiosity yourself by honoring it in your child and modeling it in your daily life.
Source: http://www.loc.gov/pictures/item/2006678019/

You probably think that you already answer your child's questions, but even the most responsive parents don't answer something like 25 percent of the time. It's easier to understand when you think of the volume of questions that children pose between the ages of two and five. Researchers estimate it's between four hundred and twelve hundred each week, depending on the child. I know that when my kids were young, my best parenting self understood I should calmly and carefully respond to every question, but there were times I whined, "Can't I just drink my coffee for five minutes?"

Here are some reasons questions might frustrate you, along with some ideas about how to cope:

She tunes out while I'm answering. Trying making answers shorter. For example, if your child says, "Why are leaves green?" you can't get into details about photosynthesis, not even a stripped-down version. Just say something like, "The food for the tree is in the leaves, and the food is green." For this age group, the briefer the answer, the better. If she wants to know more, she'll ask. (Data-free speculation on my part: dads seem much more prone to give inappropriately long answers to kids' questions than moms.)

She tunes out before I've answered. Sometimes a child seems to throw questions at you without listening to the answers, for example, asking "Why?" in response to everything you say. It's tempting to close down the endless loop by saying, "You're not really listening." Instead, try posing a question of your own. Turning the same question back to the child usually won't get you very far ("Why do *you* think leaves are green?"). Instead, try a question to which the child knows the answer, for example, "Why is your table red?" Answer: "Because we painted it." "So do you think someone painted the leaves?" You may end up in a quite different conversation, but that's fine.

She keeps asking the same thing again and again. It's not necessarily the case that she's a bad listener or has a bad memory. She may simply have not understood the answer very well the last time you explained it. Or more likely, you've answered what she seemed to ask, but she had a different question in mind.

I should know the answer but don't. "Why is the sky blue?" *I know I learned that at some point . . .* ! If you have no idea what the right answer is, say so. Validate that the question is interesting and ask the child to help you remember that the two of you will look up the answer later. Even for young children, I see no reason that the responsibility for remembering to check the answer should not be shared. You're telling your child, "You're curious—great! You can be the agent to satisfy your curiosity!"

When I look up the answer, she gets distracted. By what? By other entries in the encyclopedia? Well, that seems kind of cool. By photos on your phone? Then don't look up answers on your phone. Learn from your child what works.

The question makes me uncomfortable. "Is Grandpa going to die from his cancer?" "How come those two men are holding hands?" "Rebecca said her religion doesn't believe in Jesus. How can that be?" Don't shut questions down that make you uncomfortable. You don't want to cordon off part of the world as unavailable for curiosity. And of course if your child senses your discomfort, this may discourage future questions on other topics. Bear in mind that he has no way of knowing which ones are off-limits. Three thoughts on this issue. First, answer the actual question posed. On sensitive topics, we have a tendency to assume our child is asking what we are afraid he'll ask rather than what he's actually asking (figure 3.3). Second, brevity is still to be prized. There is no need to tell him more than he asked. Third, if your child is unsatisfied with your brief answer and persists, requesting facts you feel he's not ready for, try saying, "I've given you some information about this, so I'd like you to think that over. Think about it, and if you still have questions, we can talk about it more later." The odds are good that he'll forget about it, but if he doesn't, you've bought yourself some time to consider how you want to discuss the matter.

Figure 3.3. Discomfiting questions. When a two-year-old asks, "Where do babies come from?" we hear a question about the sex act, but that's not what he's asking. An answer like, "They grow inside a mommy's body, near where food is in her tummy," is probably all he's looking for at that moment.
Source: © Jordan Fischer, via Flickr, Creative Common License. https://www.flickr.com/photos /jordanfischer/483114005/.

If you like the idea of your kids asking you questions and showing curiosity about the world, there is something you can do to cultivate it: ask *them* questions. Researchers have found that some parents talk to their kids mostly with directions about what to do ("Go to bed") and what not to do ("Stop that"). Other parents engage in much more communication by question ("It's Tuesday—where do you think we're going after school?"). Naturally every parent does some of each, but individuals seem to lean toward one type or the other and in so doing set up a model for their child regarding the nature of communication. If you give a lot of commands, you're showing your child that the purpose of language is for communicating one's wishes to others. If you ask a lot of questions, you're showing your child that the purpose of language is the acquisition of new knowledge.

Some researchers have also suggested that question-asking parents tend to invite conversation even when they tell their children what to do. They do so by offering reasons along with their requests, and a reason invites a counterargument. For example, a parent might say, "You had better go to bed now, or you'll be too tired to get up in time for school." The child can then try to subvert the reason: "But remember, last week I stayed up until 9:30 and I wasn't tired the next morning." In contrast, the parent who simply says, "Go to bed," offers no opening for the child to bargain or reason for a later bedtime.

READING ALOUD

When you think of activities parents might undertake to develop their child's knowledge, reading aloud is probably high on your list (figure 3.4). Indeed, there's good evidence that read-alouds help toddlers gain broader vocabulary and understand more complex syntax. Why? Think about the

Figure 3.4. Reading aloud. When the National Academy of Education commissioned a report on reading in 1985 written by ten prominent reading researchers, they named reading aloud as the most important activity to get more kids reading.
Source: © Alex Tihonov—Fotolia. For the report, see Anderson (1985).

language that children overhear in the conversations of their parents. Even preschoolers' books have richer vocabulary than that used by college-educated adults in typical conversation. Furthermore, conversations are full of interruptions and unfinished sentences, and when the sentences are complete, the syntax is usually quite simple.

Since we're talking about building background knowledge, it seems natural that we'd think about including nonfiction in read-alouds. It's a great idea. It lets your child know that books are not *only* narratives and there are terrific nonfiction selections available. As always, I'd be sensitive to what your child likes. If my fabulous book about pond life made my child cry for *Curious George*, I'd read her *Curious George*. But I'd try a different nonfiction book a couple of days later.

Read-alouds don't help children learn how to read when they get to kindergarten, but again, we wouldn't expect them to. In kindergarten children are learning to decode. The benefit of reading aloud is a benefit to the child's knowledge and vocabulary, and so it appears only around grade 3 or 4.

How Do You Get Started?

There's no reason not to read to a newborn, and by "newborn" I mean just home from the hospital. (That's what the American Academy of Pediatrics recommends.) At the same time, while reading may be a nice reason to hold your baby, you should probably be aware that he can't really see much of the book. At birth, babies' vision is 20/500 (meaning they can see at twenty feet what an adult with good vision sees at five hundred feet.) They also don't have typical color vision until three months (they can't see blues), and it's at that age that they start to be able to focus better. Furthermore, babies are much more social at three months than at three days. So for my money, three months is a good time to begin reading to them.

The main (or, really, only) thing I was doing with my infant children when I read to them was establishing a bedtime ritual—something we both enjoyed and that helped them wind down and understand that it was time to sleep. So it was a simple matter of propping the child in my lap, holding the book so she could see it, and reminding myself that it was okay if she didn't really pay attention or started chewing the book. If you set more ambitious goals for reading to an infant, you might think that the child is

Figure 3.5. Learning vocabulary from picture books. If you want your very young child to learn vocabulary from read-alouds (which was never one of my goals), your best bet is a book with one object per page. Read the label while pointing to the object. Just say "cat." Not, "Look, there's a cat. You have a cat too, don't you? Look this one is gray but yours is brown, isn't it?" If you're interested in your child learning something, make plain what is to be learned.
Source: © Wichittra Srisunon—Fotolia.

getting exposed to some vocabulary or that you're laying the groundwork for the alphabetic principle (the idea that letters represent sounds) and that the book is guiding what Daddy says (figure 3.5).

Dialogic Reading

If you're really concerned about maximizing the chances that your child will learn from read-alouds, you can consider using another technique, *dialogic reading*. You'll recall that print referencing (discussed in the previous chapter) was meant to teach kids about letters. Dialogic reading makes it more likely that kids will learn new vocabulary and more complex sentence syntax from read-alouds. The steps of dialogic reading form an acronym, PEER:

> **P**rompt the child to say something about the book.
> **E**valuate the child's response.
> **E**xpand the child's response with new information.
> **R**epeat the prompt.

Say you're reading a picture book and there is a barnyard scene. You might point to a tractor and ask, "What's that?" (the Prompt). The child replies, "It's a truck." You say, "Yes, it's a type of truck" (the Evaluation). "That type of truck is called a tractor" (the Expansion). "Can you say tractor?" (the Repetition).

There are lots of different prompts you might use; not all prompts ask the child to identify something. You might ask the child to relate something in the book to his own experience. You might ask him to describe what's happening in the picture. You can ask at the end of a book what happened to one of the characters.

Some parents find dialogic reading a bit formal. I understand; it does feel a bit teachy and as if it might take some of the fun out of read-alouds. Still, you should know that it's been thoroughly studied, and dialogic reading reliably has a big impact. Not only does it show more benefit to kids' language ability than simply reading aloud; the latter often doesn't show much positive impact at all. I believe the research, but it should be borne in mind that these studies are of relatively short duration. I suspect that reading aloud, even if it's casually done, is still of value over the long term. So if dialogic reading really rubs you the wrong way, don't feel that's the only way you can read to your two-year-old. Or do dialogic reading on occasion to feel it out; or your child may like it more than you think.

Commonsense Read-Aloud Tips

Even if you're not going to use a prescribed method of reading aloud, I think some principles are worth your consideration. Here are some *non-research-based* ideas on reading to a toddler or preschooler:

Preparation

1. Having a consistent time for reading will help ensure that it actually happens. Before bed is a natural, but if that doesn't work for your family, find another time. Maybe Dad reads aloud while Mom cooks dinner, or vice versa.

2. There are terrific resources to help you find books for read-alouds, and I've listed some in the "Suggestions for Further Reading" section at the end of this book. But the best resource is a children's librarian. Librarians not only have a comprehensive knowledge of children's literature, they can help pick books based on your child's interests and based on the sort of book that your child liked in the past.

3. When selecting books, be alert to themes that may make your child uncomfortable (e.g., books that are emotionally intense).

4. Don't neglect your own preferences. My daughters liked the Amelia Bedelia books, but I couldn't stand them. I was a better reading dad with other books so I picked other books.

5. Bring home *lots* of books from the library so that you can quit a book your child doesn't like.

Reading

1. If you want to snuggle, you'll probably position the book so your child can see the pictures. If not, consider *facing* your child so he can't see the pictures as you read. Instead, you read what's on the page and then turn the book so he can see the pictures. That way he's focusing on one thing at a time (story, then pictures).

2. Point out the title and the name of the author and illustrator.

3. Read a little more slowly than you think you need to. Remember that even simple stories are probably cognitively challenging for your child. For that reason, don't balk if your child wants to hear the same story again and again. It may well be that he simply didn't get all the details on the first or even the third listening. If the repetition drives you crazy, suggest that you alternate the favorite book with a new one.

4. Don't demand perfect behavior (toddlers are gonna squirm), but if your child is obviously not listening, just stop reading. Don't say, "Settle down!" or, "I can't read it you're not paying attention." Just wait. If he doesn't care that you've stopped, ask if he'd rather hear another book.

5. If your child is a habitual squirmer, consider asking her to act out the actions described in the story. That may provide an outlet for movement while keeping her mind on the narrative.

6. If he wants to hold the book or turn the pages, let him, even if it makes it hard for you to read. He'll probably focus more on the page turning than the story, but this will be a phase that won't last long.

7. If you get into a book and feel it's too hard—long descriptive passages, lots of unfamiliar words—edit as you read. You can also stop and summarize something for your child. Or ask her if she understands what just happened.

8. Use a dramatic voice. Ham it up. Don't be self-conscious. Your child is not judging you (figure 3.6).

Figure 3.6. Ham it up. If you don't seem enthusiastic about and interested in the story, why should your child be?
Source: © Gail Lovette.

Electronic Books for Read-Alouds

Is a read-aloud any different with an electronic book? Studies have compared children listening to an audio version of a book with reading a paper version or e-book with a parent. The outcome measures might be story comprehension, or improvements in hearing speech sounds, or better knowledge of letters. Some studies show e-readers superior to paper, some show them inferior, and some show no difference. Some studies indicate that parents and children interact differently when reading an electronic book together, although the impact is not consistently good or bad for the child.

Why are the data all over the place? Very likely because e-books for kids can take so many forms. For example, suppose that when the child touches a picture of an animal, its name is spelled on the screen. That might boost letter awareness if the letter-sound pairs are simple ("dog") but not if they aren't (e.g., "jaguar"). This interactive feature might contribute to story comprehension if drawing attention to the animal helped the child make sense of the narrative. If not, it might be a distraction that detracts from comprehension.

. . . .

There's just one problem with all the advice I've been offering about reading aloud. I've been assuming that the idea pleases your child. What if he's not interested? It's time to turn our attention to the question of motivation.

Keeping It Simple Summary

- Don't simplify your vocabulary too much.
- Answer questions.
- Pose questions.
- Read aloud.

NOTES

"Infants as young as 9 months show this response": Junge, Cutler, and Hagoort (2012); Parise and Csibra (2012).

"children mirror the type of talk that they hear": Weizman and Snow (2001); Zimmerman et al. (2009).

"I'm suggesting that you pay attention to how you talk to your kids": Landry et al. (2012).

"two-thirds of the questions that kids around this age pose are meant to elicit information": Chouinard, Harris, and Maratsos (2007).

"it's between four hundred and twelve hundred each week, depending on the child": Chouinard et al. (2007).

"you're showing your child that the purpose of language is the acquisition of new knowledge": Tizard and Hughes (1984).

"question-asking parents tend to invite conversation even when they tell their children what to do": Lareau (2003).

"read-alouds help toddlers gain broader vocabulary and understand more complex syntax": Hood, Conlon, and Andrews (2008).

"it appears only around grade 3 or 4": Dickinson, Golinkoff, and Hirsh-Pasek (2010).

"consider using another technique, *dialogic reading*": Arnold and Whitehurst (1994); Zevenbergen and Whitehurst (2003).

"more likely that kids will learn new vocabulary and more complex sentence syntax from read-alouds": Justice and Pullen (2003); Mol, Bus, de Jong, and Smeets (2008).

"e-readers superior to paper": For research concluding that e-readers are superior to paper, see Korat, Segal-Drori, and Klien (2009); Segal-Drori, Korat, Shamir, and Klein (2009).

"some show them inferior": For research showing them to be inferior, see de Jong and Bus (2002); Matthew (1997); and Trushell, Burrell, and Maitland (2001).

"some show no difference": For research showing no difference, see de Jong and Bus (2004); Korat and Or (2010); and Korat and Shamir (2007).

"parents and children interact differently when reading an electronic book": Parish-Morris, Mahajan, Hirsh-Pasek, and Golinkoff (2011); Segal-Drori et al. (2009).

4

SEEING THEMSELVES AS READERS BEFORE THEY CAN READ

Raising a reader arguably begins and ends with motivation. If the child lacks decoding skills or the background knowledge to support comprehension, she'll gain them through reading, and if she's motivated, she'll read.

In chapter 1, I noted that motivation is fueled by positive attitudes and a concept of oneself as a reader. But the catch is that your child needs to read (and to enjoy reading) to develop a positive attitude and a solid reading self-concept. In this chapter, we examine two strategies: ways you can improve reading attitudes and self-concept without your child reading and ways to get your child to choose reading as an activity.

INDIRECT INFLUENCES

Emotional attitudes—whether I like or hate fruitcake, for example—seem self-evidently to be a product of our experience. We taste it, we react, and there's our attitude. Self-concept too is driven by experience. If we repeatedly choose to eat it, "proud fruitcake eater" may become part of our self-concept. Your child's attitude toward reading and learning new things is likewise shaped by direct experience with books and learning. But attitudes and self-concept are subject to indirect influences as well.

Indirect Influences on Attitudes

Direct experiences can't be the only source of emotional attitudes. If they were, how could you explain the attitudes of people who say they love

Coke but hate Pepsi? Really, does anyone drink Coke and think *yum yum*, but should he drink a Pepsi by mistake think, *Good God, this is vile!*? (If you need proof, you'll like a study in which experimenters put Coke in a Pepsi bottle and vice versa; it turned out that people picked their "favorite" beverage based on the bottle label, not on the content.) The emotion in these attitudes comes not from experience of the products but from emotional reactions to other objects that become associated with the product. Think about what Coke emphasizes in its advertising: that it tastes good, sure. Even more, the ads seek to create associations between Coke and things that consumers already like: young love, cute polar bears, Santa Claus, and (of course) attractive people.

When you spell out the psychological mechanism behind these ads, it sounds kind of creepy. It's the same as the one in Pavlov's famous experiment with the salivating dog. The dog salivates when it eats. If you ring a bell just before you feed the dog (and repeat this a few dozen times), the dog will come to salivate when it hears the bell. Advertisers are not interested in salivation but in positive emotions. A cool, funny, muscular guy in a towel prompts positive emotions in many viewers. Pair that guy with Old Spice enough times, and Old Spice becomes associated with positive emotions. It seems blatantly manipulative, and we think it wouldn't work on us, but it does.

Reading attitudes are fostered in part by these sorts of associations. When I see a childhood favorite in a bookstore, I feel the warm glow of nostalgia. *Winnie-the-Pooh* or *Horton Hears a Hoo* makes me think of my mother reading to me at bedtime. Seeing *Mrs. Piggle Wiggle* or a Beverly Cleary book reminds me of the pride I felt in getting my first library card and being allowed to walk to the library on my own. That warm glow is a Pavlovian response. And indeed, research shows that positive childhood experiences with books are associated with later reading.

I'm not going to suggest you have a muscular, funny guy in a towel wander about your house, reading Homer, and muttering "fascinating . . . fascinating." But the idea of reading being associated with warm bedtime snuggles seems practicable. So does arranging a cozy reading corner (figure 4.1). How about setting aside a time that the family reads together for fifteen minutes, each member with his or her own book? Maybe this reading time includes indulging in a special drink, which changes with the season.

Figure 4.1. Reading corners. My youngest daughter has a dormer in her room, which makes for an ideal reading spot. Her older sister lacks a dormer but makes up for it with the child-sized armchair.
Source: ©Daniel Willingham.

One of the best ways to cement this positive attitude toward reading and learning about the world is through family traditions—things that your family makes a point of doing time and time again. Family traditions reveal what you value enough to repeat, and—if done with love—build warm, happy associations. For example, my parents kept a dictionary in the kitchen and the encyclopedia a few steps away. It was a rare day that one or the other was not consulted during a kitchen table conversation. Teenaged me would sometimes roll my eyes at my nerdy parents. Doesn't "enclose" mean the same thing as "envelop"? Who cares whether Lincoln ever served in the Senate? But I got the message: words matter, knowledge matters. And, yeah, I keep a dictionary in my kitchen now.

Here are a few other examples of family rituals:

- The family that went for a walk on the first day of each new season, rain or shine, even if it had to be brief. They would note, discuss, and appreciate the changes in nature.
- The family that read the newspaper together every Sunday morning, reading aloud bits of articles they enjoyed.
- The family that ensured that *every* birthday (for adults too) included at least one book as a present. (New hardbacks are expensive, but there is a robust market in used children's books.)
- The parents who, each New Year's morning, let the children present a list of suggested spots for the next summer's family vacation, with the proviso that every city named had to have a museum.
- The family that made weekly trips to the library, where the kids were allowed to read to their heart's content and bring home as many books as they liked.
- The parents who, deciding that their kids had enough "stuff," instituted a tradition that for birthdays, grandparents would record a book for the birthday child.

Indirect Influences on Self-Concept

In chapter 1, I wrote that our self-concept comes from our behavior. It's as though we watch ourselves and note how we are different from other people: *Gee, I seem to read a lot, compared to most people I know*. But reading a lot is not the only way to build a reading self-concept, especially when children are young. Parents communicate to children what they value as a family—what's important in life.

I think these messages—"our family is like *this*"—are enormously important, and kids perceive and understand them early. Two-year-olds want to figure out how kids and adults differ. Five-year-olds perceive that families differ in their habits and practices. They discover that "finish your dinner before you get dessert" is not a rule set by adults; it's a rule in my family, and Robert's parents (God bless them) don't follow that rule. Those differences prompt comparison—my house versus other houses—and so become another source of the child's self-image.

Sometimes the message is quite direct. I remember visiting a friend's house when I was perhaps ten and, spying a decorative dish in the living room, I pointed out to him that it was empty and that it really ought to hold candy. He thought that was an excellent idea and brought it to his mother. She said with cool derision, "We are not the type of people who put out candy in dishes." The message clearly went far beyond candy: "This is well-bred family, and we do not engage in behaviors that might indicate otherwise." (The missing piece for me is why a public display of candy signals the hoi polloi, but I guess a well-bred person would know not to ask such a question.)

So how can you show your child that reading and learning new things are family values? An obvious implication is that your child should see you reading. Telling your child to do something you neglect yourself won't work (figure 4.2).

Figure 4.2. Be a model. In one of Aesop's fables, a mother crab chides her child to walk forward instead of sideways. The child responds, "Please show me how, and I will follow." The thought is still relevant more than twenty-five hundred years later. You can't tell your child "go read" while you are watching television or checking Instagram.
Source: © Wenceslaus Hollar, via Wikimedia Commons.

There are other ways to signal its importance. You can display books prominently in your home. You can ensure that your child has her own bookcase and collection of books, however modest. Once your child is old enough, you can insist that books be treated as objects of respect. It might be tolerable for a doll to be tossed on the floor when a more interesting activity beckons, but books must be put away with care.

In addition to showing your child that you love to read, modeling means showing your child that you are interested in learning about the world and are always curious to learn something new. I touched on this when I pointed out that it's not only important to answer your child's questions thoughtfully, but also to pose your own questions to your child. And there are, of course, destinations meant to encourage curiosity—zoos, children's museums, and the like. By all means, take advantage of them. And if you go, model curiosity by reading the information placards, not just looking at the animals or pushing the button to see the lightning bolt jump between the electrodes.

Wonderful as such excursions are, I think it's more important to model curiosity in daily activities so as not to compartmentalize it as a special event. See a new fruit in the grocery store? Try it. Watching a ball game? Wonder aloud how often double plays happen. See an interesting bug? Snap a picture on your phone and try to identify it when you get home. Traveling somewhere for business? Find out a little about the town, even if you know you won't have time to see the sights.

GETTING YOUNG CHILDREN TO READ

We've explored ways to promote positive reading attitudes and positive reading self-concepts other than having the child read. The motivation for doing that is a seeming conundrum: positive attitudes and self-concepts are prompted by positive reading experiences, but why would the child read if she doesn't already have a positive reading attitude? In this section, we consider the idea that attitudes are not the only guide for what we do and what we refrain from doing. Other factors contribute, and parents can make use of them to get kids reading.

How Do We Choose?

When we think about getting reluctant kids on board with reading, our focus is often on finding a great book. We hope the appeal of the book will overwhelm the child's indifferent attitude, and then, once the child enjoys the book, his attitude will change for the better. But any choice, including "Should I read this book?" is influenced by multiple factors, not just the book's appeal. To give you some sense of these factors, have a look at these questions, and answer each in your mind as you read:

Question 1: I offer you the choice of a 1.5 ounce chocolate bar OR $3 million. Which do you choose?

Question 2: I offer you the choice of a 1.5 ounce chocolate bar that you are certain to get OR a lottery scratch ticket with a prize of $3 million. The odds of winning the jackpot are 1 in 5 million.

Question 3: I offer you the choice of a 1.5 ounce chocolate bar that you are certain to get OR a lottery scratch ticket with a prize of $3 million. The odds of winning the jackpot are 1 in 5 million. If you pick the scratch ticket, you'll get it immediately, but if you pick the chocolate bar, you'll have to wait a month and drive to the next town to pick it up.

Question 4: I offer you a 1.5 ounce chocolate bar. Do you take it?

When I wrote these examples, my thought was that your choice would change between the chocolate bar and lottery ticket each time I added a new element to the choice. My point was to illustrate four factors that I'll suggest go into choices, whether it's picking a caterer for your wedding, deciding whether to walk the dog or watch TV, or choosing whether to read a book or play a video game.

The first question—chocolate bar or $3 million—highlights the anticipated outcome. If I make this choice, what do I think I'll get? I choose to do things that offer outcomes I like, of course, and that's what's on our mind when we look for books that we hope our kids will like.

But when people make choices, they don't just think about the outcomes, because they recognize they may not actually get the outcome they anticipate. When I change the $3 million to a lottery ticket that's potentially worth $3 million (but probably won't win), we have an extreme example of this principle—very desirable outcome but very small odds of actually getting it—and so the modest but certain reward of the chocolate bar might hold greater appeal. Think of how a child might consider the odds when she chooses to read. Imagine an elementary school student who loved the movie *Despicable Me*. She's with her father in the bookstore and he points out an early-reader novel based on the movie. She's quite confident that this book would in principle offer a lot of pleasure. But she may doubt that she has the skills to read it. She views the book the way you view a lottery ticket.

The third question (in which I said you'd have to wait a month to get the chocolate bar) underscores still another factor that goes into choices. Sometimes an outcome looks desirable and we're pretty sure we'll get it, but making the associated choice incurs a cost we're not willing to pay. I'd choose a Cadillac over my Kia, but I don't because of the cost. One rather obvious way that readers must "pay up" is in the attention the book requires, a function of the difficulty of the text relative to the reader's skill. We want reading material that poses a modest challenge. Another cost is the effort I must expend to get access to the book (figure 4.3).

A somewhat more subtle cost is time, that is, having to wait. The value of something nice declines if we know we'll have to wait for it. For example, if you ask me at noon whether I want dessert after supper, it's pretty easy for me to say, "No, I'm trying to lose a few pounds." But if you offer me cake just after we've finished supper, it's much harder to say no. Cake *now* has more reward value than cake I'm contemplating having a few hours from now. The implication for reading is that we want ready access to books. When a child is in the mood to read, she should not have to wait even a few hours to get to the book.

The final question, in which I offered only the chocolate bar, is meant to highlight that reading is not a choice made in isolation. This offer—have it or not—seems realistic for chocolate bars, but the child does not compare reading a book to doing nothing. The child compares reading to something else he might do: read *Bridge to Terabithia* or, say, play the

Figure 4.3. We're lazier than we think. You may know that manufacturers pay grocery stores to put their products on more desirable shelves, and no shelf is more desirable than the one at eye level. This is an example of accessibility affecting choice. It's hard to believe, but simply having to move our eyes up or down constitutes a cost to finding products. To maximize the chances your child will read, you want to have books so easy to access he will almost stumble over them.
Source: © Art Allianz—Fotolia.com.

video game *Portal*. So it's not enough that the child regards reading as an attractive choice. Reading must be the most attractive choice available at the moment the decision is made. This is an enormously important consideration. The average high schooler doesn't hate reading, yet he virtually never chooses to read because there is always another activity available that is more appealing.

I've suggested that four factors go into whether the child will choose to read a book: (1) the pleasure she thinks the book might offer, (2) her judgment as to the likelihood that she'll actually experience that pleasure if she tries to read it, (3) what cost she anticipates that reading the book would incur, (4) and what she might choose to do instead of read. Throughout this book, we'll focus on ways to maximize each factor: finding books that your child is likely to enjoy, boosting your child's reading self-confidence, and making access to books easier.

Making Reading the Most Attractive Choice

Because this chapter is about prereaders looking at picture books, some of the concerns we have with older children are not relevant. For prereaders, you don't have to worry too much about picking just the right book or that the child frets about his reading competence. Your focus should be on making reading the most attractive choice available.

The simplest way to start is to make sure that she has access to books in places where she would otherwise be bored. Put a basket of books in the bathroom. Put another in the kitchen. Better than a basket is a bookcase that displays titles. That way your child can see what's available, and especially at this age, book covers are more enticing than book spines (figure 4.4).

Always have a book or two with you when you are running errands for moments when you get stuck in a line. Put a basket of books in the car, ideally in a spot your child can reach from his car seat. One destination for these errands should be the library—weekly or biweekly if you can. Regular visits allow you to fill your bookcases at no cost, and they are a great place to find a cozy corner on a cold winter's day or to linger in cool quiet during the heat of summer. And lingering in a place with a lot of books will likely lead to reading.

Figure 4.4. Display bookcases. These bookcases allow kids to easily see what's available. The design on the left is wall mounted and takes up little room, so it's a good choice for kitchens or bathrooms.

Source: © Steffy Wood Products, Inc. Used by permission.

Keeping Screen Time under Control

Access to books is important, but it's not enough. Most kids will choose screens—"screens" generically referring to video content, games, or computer applications—over a book, even a readily available one. For reasons I don't understand, moving images on a screen entrance. We stare at them as we stare at flames or ocean waves. I've never met a parent who said, "Yeah, he watched television a couple of times, but he really wasn't interested."

Very young children—those in their first two years of life—spend twice as much time watching television and videos as they do being read to (fifty-three versus twenty-three minutes per day). Slightly older children (aged five to eight years) watch more television than younger kids do (about two hours per day) although they read or are read to about the same amount of time (thirty-three minutes per day). At this age, children start to use other digital devices: 90 percent have used a computer at least once, and 22 percent use a computer daily. For console video games, the figures are only slightly lower. The use of these other devices, along with greater television viewing, means that the average five- to eight-year-old is exposed to about three hours forty-five minutes of various media each day. By the time kids are in their late teens, average media exposure approaches *eleven hours per day.*

My guess is that very few parents are happy that their teens spend so much time with digital devices. I'm also guessing those parents didn't see it coming when their kids were toddlers. But as any parent knows, it's easier to limit something at an early age than to wait until it's a problem and then try to change course. Obviously some video content is more enriching than others—*Sesame Street* is not equivalent to *Tom and Jerry* cartoons—but if you want your child to be a reader, controlling the content of screen time probably won't be enough. You have to control the amount.

But many parents see screens as a lifesaver when their kids are very young. Imagine the frequency of the following scenario. Mom and Dad have both worked a long day. Their four-year-old has had a long day himself. He's hungry, frazzled, whiny. If he watches a video, he's satisfied, and twenty minutes are now available to get some supper on the table. People often describe digital technologies as offering instant gratification for kids. They are instant gratification for parents too.

Sure, any parent feels sheepish about using the television as a babysitter, but most of us have done so. And let's not catastrophize the situation: it's a twenty-minute video. The concern is how parents get from there to a child consuming hours of digital content per day. You need a two-pronged strategy to keep screen time under control: setting limits and promoting independence. Here are a few ideas on setting limits on screen time:

- **A minutes-per-day time limit is an obvious policy.** Let your child choose when to watch if that works for you, but don't be afraid to regulate when he gets his screen time if the times he chooses don't work for you too.
- **Think about making the times that your child watches videos or plays computer games regular.** If you say "three hours per week," keeping track of how much she's watched becomes a bookkeeping headache, and you end up in too many debates about how much time she has left.
- **Don't put a television or computer in your child's room.**
- **Don't put a DVD player in your car.** (Audio books are a great substitute.) If you already have a DVD player, use it only on long trips.
- **If your child has a playdate, mention to the other parents that you're trying to limit screen time,** and you hope they won't be watching videos or playing computer games. You won't sound like a fanatic. In my experience, most parents agree it's kind of silly to have a friend over and then just sit and watch television. But at the same time, if you say nothing, the kids may choose to watch a DVD, and if the house rules are "anything goes," the parents won't redirect the kids.
- **Stick to your guns.** The hardest part of limiting screen time is the whining.
- **When your children get too old for an afternoon nap, institute "quiet time."** That means your child plays quietly for an hour in his room. There are no restrictions on what he can or can't do, but it must be quiet. An hour of peace in the middle of a hectic, noisy day is a godsend for a parent, and it's also good practice for your child to learn to entertain himself.

That last idea may strike you as unrealistic. If your child drops his afternoon nap at, say, age four, will he really be able to play quietly on his own for an hour? He probably can, but he'll need your help.

Teaching Independence

Being resourceful about entertaining oneself is a skill like any other. Children must learn it, and you can actively promote this learning. That's the second prong in your strategy to limit screen time. Kids need to know that they can depend on themselves—not a screen, not a parent—for entertainment.

For crawlers and toddlers, make sure that the house is meticulously babyproofed so you don't feel that you have to watch them like a hawk. Then again, *do* watch your child like a hawk, but do so to learn what interests him. If you're trying to build independence, you need to know what he finds absorbing. I once saw a mom encouraging her twelve-month-old to play with Play-Doh, but he was having none of it. He kept fooling with the Play-Doh canisters. She finally realized that he was intrigued by how the top fit. She ditched the Play-Doh, got out half a dozen Tupperware containers, and he was happy for about thirty minutes as he removed and replaced the tops.

When setting your child up for independent play, focus on one activity at a time. If she's got an idea of what she wants to do, great. If not, try to involve her in what you're doing. A toddler can hold a dustpan while you sweep, or a bowl while you mix, and it takes no more than this sort of job for her to feel she's helping. A three-year-old can tear lettuce for a salad or stack books on a shelf. A four-year-old can set a table or water houseplants. It won't be long before your child doesn't want to help around the house, but at this age, kids are eager to do so. Of course it's faster and easier to do it yourself (and you won't make a mess), but it's worth putting in the effort to teach them (figure 4.5).

Not only will it take effort, it will take time. Think of building your child's independence in stages. Initially expect that you'll be sitting nearby engaged in your own activity and your child will frequently check in with you. She'll ask a question or request help. My basic strategy is to respond as briefly as possible. If she wants me to engage in the task with her,

Figure 4.5. Independence. Sometimes it's impossible for your child to help you in what you're doing, for example, when you're writing or using a mattock in your garden. In that case, suggest that he do something similar. If you're writing, he's coloring. If you're gardening, he's watering plants.
Source: © Chris Parfitt via Flickr.

I say, "I'm doing this now. And you know what? It looks like you're doing great with that. How about you continue, and we'll check in with each other in a few minutes?" (To be clear, I'm not saying I *never* interact with my kids. I'm talking about times when I'm self-consciously trying to build independence.)

Because building independence is a process, you should have higher expectations for your child's resourcefulness as she gets older. When my six-year-old says, "I'm bored," I'll suggest four or five things she might do. If she doesn't bite, I say, "Well, that's what I've got for you." Usually she finds something to occupy herself. If she drapes herself across the sofa and moans, "There's nothing to dooooooooo," I tell her that she's free to moan in her room but not near me.

One final thought on goals. Other parents have usually reacted to the screen restrictions in my home with a shrug, but I occasionally hear a slightly sharp edge in a friend's voice as he says something like, "You can't protect them forever," or "They'll see it at other kids' houses, you know." My goal is not that my child never sees a screen. My goal is to make space for reading, so that by the time she's ten, reading is so firmly socketed in her life that it cannot be threatened by an obsession with gossip websites, the latest video game, or anything else.

. . . .

In most schools, kindergarten marks the beginning of earnest reading instruction. In the next chapter, we begin our discussion of this age.

Keeping It Simple Summary

- Be a model of love of reading and love of knowledge.
- Communicate in words and actions that reading and learning about the world are family values.
- Change the environment to make reading the most attractive activity available.

Notes

"based on the bottle label, not on the content": Woolfolk, Castellan, and Brooks (1983).

"Old Spice becomes associated with positive emotions": Stuart, Shimp, and Engle (1984).

"positive childhood experiences with books are associated with later reading": Baker, Scher, and Mackler (1997); Rowe (1991); Walberg and Tsai (1985).

"and so become another source of the child's self-image": DeBaryshe (1995); Evans, Shaw, and Bell (2000).

"they recognize they may not actually get the outcome they anticipate": In the research literature, these are called expectancy value theories (e.g., Wigfield & Eccles, 2000).

"average media exposure approaches *eleven hours per day*": Rideout, Foehr, and Roberts (2010).

PART II

KINDERGARTEN THROUGH SECOND GRADE

5

LEARNING TO DECODE

The period from kindergarten to second grade is an age of rapid change for your reading child. In this chapter, we look at how decoding is likely taught at your school and what you can do to support your child's learning at home.

WHAT'S HAPPENING AT SCHOOL

You may have heard of what is referred to as the "reading wars," a vociferous and nasty set of arguments about the best way to teach children to read. Some background on the two instructional methods that shaped the reading wars battleground will help you understand what's happening in your child's classroom today, and you'll see that neither side fully prevailed in the war. Most children today are taught reading using a compromise method.

Two Traditional Methods of Teaching Reading

I've emphasized that the alphabet is a code that puts sounds into visual form. An essential part of reading is the process of decoding, of turning the visual forms back into sound. To understand what you read, you use the same mental machinery you draw on to comprehend spoken language; reading, in a sense, is a process of talking to oneself.

That makes it sound as though the teaching of reading ought to be uncontroversial: you teach kids the code. You plan instruction to introduce the letter-sound relationships and do so in a particular order, teaching the most common letter-sound pairs first. The umbrella term for this strategy is *phonics instruction.*

There are variants within this broad approach. Some people favor teaching the letter-sound pairs in isolation. Show the child the letter "o" and say, "This makes the sound AW, as in the word MOP." An alternative is to teach letter-sound correspondences in the context of real words. Thus, instead of telling the child that the letter combination "ou" is usually said as OW, the teacher might introduce the words "cloud," "mouse," and "found" to help the child deduce the relationship.

The competitor idea on teaching reading holds that phonics instruction is largely unnecessary. This notion is at least two hundred years old, appearing in a French monograph from 1787, *The True Way to Learning Any Language Dead or Alive* by Benoît Morin. Morin points out that when you teach a child the name of an object—a shirt, say—you don't list the parts, telling the child, "These are the buttons, here are the cuffs," and so on. No, you tell the child, "It's a shirt." Likewise, Morin says, "Hide from them all the ABCs. Entertain them with whole words which they can understand and which they will retain with far more ease and pleasure than all the printed letters." Some fifty years later, American education pioneer Horace Mann agreed that "the advantages of teaching children by beginning with whole words are many." He referred to isolated letters as "skeleton-shaped, bloodless, ghostly apparitions" and remarked it was little wonder children felt deathlike when confronted by them (figure 5.1).

Both Morin and Mann suggested that learning to read is natural. Indeed, they thought that it's as natural as learning to speak, a suggestion still put forward today by some theorists, although they are very much in the minority. The argument suggests that what makes it unnatural and difficult is the process of drilling children in letters. Instead, we should immerse children in reading and writing tasks that are pleasurable and authentic. Give the child experience with reading that makes sense to him, that has a clear point to it, and he'll be motivated to engage with it and will learn to read more or less effortlessly. An analogy is that children don't need instruction to learn to speak. They are surrounded by spoken language that carries meaning and obviously has value, and so they learn to speak. In this scheme, children will learn to read from the shapes of

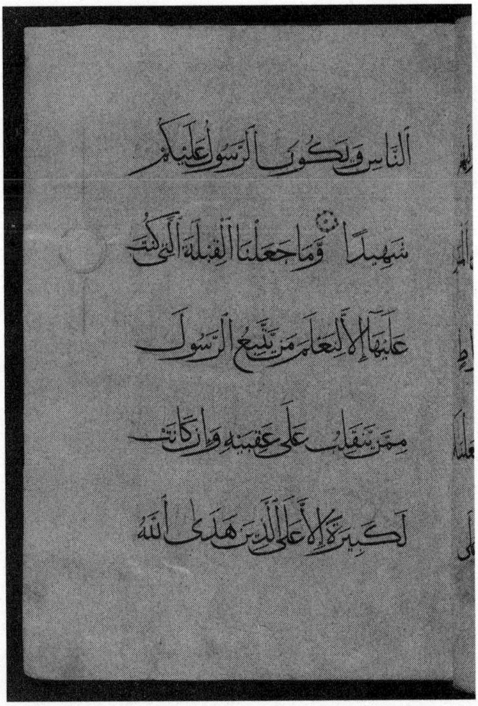

Figure 5.1. Intimidating script. Mann's description of letters as skeleton-shaped may seem a bit over the top, but when we examine a script that is alien to us—for most English speakers, *muhaqqaq*, a form of calligraphic Arabic, is an example—the script looks, if not macabre, at least intimidating.

Source: Wikimedia Commons, http://commons.wikimedia.org/wiki/File:Egyptian-_Text_Page_from _Chapter_2_-_Walters_W5614A_-_Full_Page.jpg.

words, not from the identity of individual letters. For that reason, it's called *whole-word* reading.

But this strategy—show kids whole words—brings a substantial disadvantage. Learning to read represents a huge task to human memory because kids must remember what each word looks like, and the average high schooler knows something like fifty thousand words. A lot of those words look similar, for example, "dog" and "bog." The phonics approach, in contrast, requires the memorization of a much, much smaller set of letter-sound pairings.

A whole-word advocate would reply that not all fifty thousand words need to be learned immediately, and we shouldn't forget that

The cat went to the house.
The kittens went, too.
We said, "Come, cat, come!
Come, kittens, come!"
We gave them milk for dinner.

LILLIAN M. ALLEN.

Figure 5.2. Meaning cues and reading. Suppose a child doesn't recognize the word "milk." A whole-word advocate would say that he could figure it out from the other words in the sentence and from the picture. A phonics advocate might reply that the word might just as easily be "cream." The only way to be sure is by decoding the word.
Source: Elson Readers, Primer (Scott, Foresman, 1920).

the printed word is just one of several cues available to the reader. You can often make a good guess about the identity of a word based on the meaning of other words in the sentence. Therefore, readers should be encouraged not to rely solely on print to read. The meaning of the text is another stream of information that can help them puzzle out a word. For beginning readers, we should use reading materials that have other supports to figuring out meaning—pictures, for example, that tell the story (figure 5.2).

If we do these things, say whole-word advocates—provide rich, authentic literary experiences; start with words, not letters; and teach children to use all the sources of information available—they will figure out the letter-sound correspondences as they go. Some children might need a little more support for this task, and we can provide more explicit instruction as the need arises. So whole-word advocates are not saying "no phonics whatsoever." They are saying that the teaching of phonics shouldn't be a driving force and focus behind the teacher's plan of instruction.

Who's Right?

There are a couple of ways to think about this controversy of teaching reading. The first is, "Which theory is right?" The second is, "What are the consequences of following one theory or the other?"

The Theory   The "Which theory is right?" question is easily answered. The whole-word theory makes a fundamental assumption that is almost certainly wrong.* Reading is not natural. "Natural" in this sense means that even though the task at hand is complicated, the human nervous system is in some way primed to learn the skill. It's more or less part of your inheritance as a human being that you will learn this skill, just as a house wren effortlessly learns its song and a lion learns to stalk.

When a skill is "natural," we expect to observe three things. First, everyone will learn the skill without great difficulty, and typically they will learn it by observation, without the need for overt instruction—after all, we're primed to learn it. Second, given that it's part of our inheritance as human beings, we expect that the skill can be observed in all cultures all over the world. Third, the proposal that our nervous system is primed to learn the skill implies that it will likely be evolutionarily old. It's just not very probable that an evolutionary adaptation would have popped up in the last few thousand years.

These three features—easily learned by everyone, observed in all cultures, and evolutionarily old—are true for some human skills: walking, talking, reaching, and appreciating social interactions, for example. But none of them is true for reading. Most people don't learn to read through

---

*Although I know it will make some theoreticians bristle, I'm using the terms "whole word" and "whole language" interchangeably. They are not identical, but both suggest that minimal phonics instruction is necessary, so they are much more alike than different.

observation alone, and there are peoples in the world without a written language. Finally, writing is not evolutionarily old. It's a cultural invention that is no more than fifty-five hundred years old.

The Consequences   The second way to address the "Which is right?" question is to examine experiments that have compared how well kids learn to read when instructed using phonics or instructed when using whole-word methods. There have been a great many such experiments, going back nearly a hundred years. Whenever there is a large volume of research, there is some opportunity for picking and choosing studies that support your position, and the debates about how to summarize this research literature have been hotly contested.

The governments of three English-speaking countries (the United States, Britain, and Australia) as well as the European Union countries all came up with the same strategy to resolve the question: blue-ribbon panels of scientists were appointed to sort through the data and write a report. All four panels came to the same conclusion: it's important to teach phonics, and to teach it in a planned, systematic way, not on an as-needed basis. Similar conclusions have been drawn by panels assembled by US scientific organizations.

Although all these reports were in agreement that phonics instruction is important, it's not as though kids taught using whole-word methods don't learn to read. In fact, if you compare their reading achievement to that of kids taught using phonics, there's a lot of overlap (figure 5.3). The advantage conferred by using phonics instead of the whole-word method is moderate, not huge.

There's a little more to the story. The average advantage to using phonics instruction is moderate, but it's not the case that each and every child does a little better with phonics than he or she would have done with whole-word instruction. The importance of phonics instruction varies depending on what the child knows when reading instruction begins. Phonics instruction is less important for kids who, when they start school, have good phonological awareness and understand that letters stand for sounds. They are likely to figure out the code with just a little support. But for kids who lack that knowledge, phonics instruction is likely to be very important.

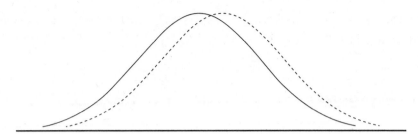

Figure 5.3. The phonics advantage. The solid line shows a typical bell curve of student reading proficiency—a few really struggle, a few read very well, and most are in the middle. The solid line shows reading proficiency when systematic phonics instruction is not part of the reading program. The dotted line shows reading proficiency when it is. You can see that phonics instruction helps, but the curves overlap quite a bit.
Source: © Daniel Willingham.

Phonics instruction has come to be seen as nonnegotiable. But even if the whole-word approach to learning to decode is flawed, the emphasis on children's literature has always seemed like a good idea to educators, and research evidence for that view accumulated through the 1980s and 1990s. It became the consensus conclusion in the late 1990s, and so was born "balanced literacy," the type of reading instruction that your child will very likely experience.

Balanced Literacy This position holds that phonics advocates were right: phonics instruction is essential. But whole-word advocates were right too: immersing children in authentic literacy activities is also crucial. And so balanced literacy was offered as a resolution to the conflict that had raged between the two approaches. Advocates also offered another allurement: they suggested that the balance might differ for different children. Thus, the theory seemed flexible, sensitive to variation among kids.

Balanced literacy suggests that phonics be taught, but in the context of an array of activities, especially ones that offer authentic literacy experiences (as opposed to, for example, completing a worksheet). The following list of K–2 activities comes from a handbook for teachers published by the New York City Department of Education. The full list includes ten other activities (for a total of sixteen), some of which would be familiar to you: teacher read-alouds, for example, and work on phonological awareness:

- **Guided reading.** The teacher works with a small group of students (no more than six) who are reading at about the same level and have similar needs. The students have individual copies of the text (preferably short selections) and independently read orally or silently as the teacher observes, coaches, prompts, and evaluates their performance. The teacher encourages students to think critically about the text.
- **Shared reading.** When a text is difficult for students to read without help, the teacher reads aloud at a rate that allows the students to join in, although usually slightly behind the teacher. The teacher models the three cueing systems of reading—phonics, grammar, and meaning—by making his or her thinking transparent by asking the children, "Does this make sense?" (meaning); "Does this sound right?" (phonics); "Does this look right?" (grammar).
- **Independent reading.** Students self-select books at their reading level and take responsibility for working through the challenges of the text independently.
- **Modeled writing.** The teacher demonstrates the act of writing by thinking aloud while composing text in front of the students.
- **Shared writing.** This can be done with the whole class or a small group. The teachers and students share the composing process. The teacher acts as the recorder. By writing down what he or she and the class want to say, the teacher reinforces concepts of print.
- **Interactive writing.** Student and teacher compose with the teacher, "sharing the pen" at strategic points. There is a greater emphasis on teaching conventions of writing (compared to shared writing).

So what does the research say? Does balanced literacy work? The quick-and-dirty answer is, "It should." We know that the pieces—phonics instruction and children's literature—work. But giving a firmer research-based answer will have to wait, for two reasons. First, balanced literacy programs are relatively new. We know that reading success is influenced by many factors, so it's hard to draw firm conclusions from individual experiments. Second, there is a lot of variation in what actually happens in a balanced literacy program. Programs vary, and kids' experiences within a program vary. Indeed, a recent survey showed that American teachers largely agreed with the tenets of balanced literacy, but there was a lot of variation in what happened in their classrooms. And increasing evidence confirms what is likely your intuition: different kids learn better from different activities, depending on the strengths and interests they bring to the classroom.

Reading Classrooms Today

National studies show that most early elementary teachers are using some version of balanced literacy (few use phonics-only or whole-language only). But associated classroom activities are hard to predict, and we don't have good research evidence bearing on which activities are best. So where does that leave us?

Classroom Activities   We are not completely in the dark as to which activities are more likely to help kids. I offer four principles from cognitive psychology that, until we have firmer research about what works, would be prudent to bear in mind as we think about classroom activities:

1. **Don't forget phonics.** The point of balanced literacy is "phonics plus rich literacy experiences." If phonics instruction is one of sixteen possible activities, you do want to guard against the possibility that they are viewed as all being equally important. Some researchers have noted that planning manuals for some balanced literacy programs allot scant time to phonics instruction and don't even list the teaching of the alphabetic principle as a goal. If the English language arts block is between 90 and 120 minutes (typical for early elementary years), I'd hope to see 20 or 25 percent devoted to phonics (i.e., twenty to thirty minutes). Naturally, this doesn't mean that all of that time must be direct instruction or quizzing. A variety of activities could provide phonics practice. But again, when kids are practicing phonics, that practice should be focused.

2. **Students can focus on only one new thing at a time.** Some literacy activities seem to demand that kids do two things at once. For example, when the teacher is composing text and thinking aloud as she does so, she's both modeling the writing process and giving the students an implicit phonics lesson. But we know from other research that kids (and adults) can't focus on two things at a time—especially two ideas that are pretty challenging. Lessons that focus on one thing at a time are more likely to be successful.

3. **You learn more from doing than watching.** As the Bateke proverb says, "You learn how to cut down trees cutting them down." When you're told to watch someone, it's easy to let your mind wander and think something else. Hence, I'm not keen on activities like shared reading, in which the students follow along while someone else reads.

4. **Feedback matters.** Corrected errors contribute to learning. Uncorrected errors do not and may contribute to an error-laden habit. Sometimes we can catch our own mistakes, but we are less likely to do so if we are less skillful. The pro knows what she did wrong; the novice does not. Hence, when children are learning to decode, silent reading is not going to be nearly as helpful as reading aloud.

Sometimes an activity is useful for purposes other than pure literacy. A first-grade teacher told me that she used the shared writing technique for about four months with a student who simply froze when asked to write anything. She wisely saw that a bit of support from her would get him past his fear. So these techniques can be put to good use. But for the typical student learning to decode, I'd hope to see (1) learning letter-sound combinations in order of frequency, (2) memorizing a small set of very common irregular words (e.g., "the," "and," "when") as sight words, (3) reading aloud, with feedback, (4) writing, and (5) lots of work with children's literature.

Going Digital   I've noted that children vary in how quickly they benefit from phonics instruction and therefore will vary in how much of it they need. Thus, we'd really like the ability to fine-tune it: if a child understands quickly, you want to move him along to more interesting stuff, but if he doesn't, he can get the instruction he needs. That sort of individualized instruction is what most teachers strive for, but it sounds hard to pull off, and it is.

Digital technologies are supposed to make this personalization possible. A computer application might titrate instruction to the child's performance. Animation and sound could put some pizzazz into important but not intrinsically interesting material, and voice recognition technology offers the promise of evaluating student responses. You can't do any of that with a worksheet, and a teacher can't do it with a whole class simultaneously.

Scores of studies have examined the impact of educational technology on reading achievement, and several research reviews have pulled this work together. Researchers have concluded that technology has a modest positive effect on reading outcomes. "Modest" means technology interventions, on average, would move a student at the 50 percentile of reading up to perhaps the 55th or 65th percentile (the estimates vary).

With all the power we attribute to technology, that seems like a pretty wimpy effect. But the modest impact is actually typical for educational technology interventions, no matter what the subject: math, science, or history. More disturbing is a point made by researcher John Hattie: when you try anything new in the classroom, you see, on average, this sort of modest boost to student learning. Why? It's not clear. (My guess is that the excitement of trying something new makes teachers enthusiastic, and that excitement rubs off on students.) The conclusion I'm emphasizing is that educational technology interventions in general (and those targeting reading in particular) have been less successful than we would have expected.

You might protest that the question, "Does technology improve reading achievement?" is a dumb one. Surely technology applications vary in quality. I think that point is exactly right. It was *possible* that the advantages of digital technology were so powerful that virtually any tool you developed would be pretty good. In fact, you still hear people talk this way. They point out (as I just did) that technology enables self-paced learning, that it enables the integration of other media like sound and video, that it enables individualized feedback. These advantages are displayed on the table, so to speak, and we are invited to take it as self-evident that technology will be a boon.

But of course those features must be implemented well. Embedded video may distract rather than intrigue, or the algorithm meant to adapt to a student's reading level may be faulty. And if we're just making a case based on what sounds plausible, we should note that teaching reading with technology also has plausible-sounding drawbacks. Technology does not

Figure 5.4. A feature-rich but confusing remote. This remote has too many buttons, and they are poorly labeled.
Source: © nito fotolia.

capitalize on the student's relationship with the teacher, a factor known to be important in early reading. In addition, broken or lost devices, software glitches, and compatibility problems are frequent headaches in many tech-heavy environments (figure 5.4).

We have learned one thing: technology alone doesn't do much. Researchers must move on to the job of sorting out when software helps, hinders, or has no effect on reading achievement. They must also sort out the likely complex interactions among these features. That will be no small job.

The current bland conclusion is that some tech products meant to teach reading are good, some are bad, and some are in between—obvious, of course—but at least we know that we shouldn't make a panicky decision to buy a reading program merely out of fear that we will be left behind the times. I know a decision made on that basis sounds foolish, but ask around and you'll meet plenty of teachers who will tell you that their school or district has made technology purchasing decisions on just that basis: "We don't want our kids to be left behind."

What to Do at Home

Helping your child on the path to reading gets a lot more complicated once she enters kindergarten. Even if you appreciate that your child's reading education is not wholly in the hands of the school, you still have to figure out how to coordinate what you're doing with what's happening in the classroom. My general take: don't be timid about doing what you think will help your child, but be sure you communicate well with your child's teacher. At the least, let her know what you're doing and partner with her if at all possible.

Reading with Your Child

You have been reading *to* your child for years. As she starts to learn to decode, you also begin to read *with* her. The idea is that she reads with some support from you. The support you offer takes two forms: you remind her how to sound out words when she needs help, and you provide emotional support and enthusiasm. One-on-one practice is quite valuable at this stage of learning, but teachers have too many students to allow much of it in the classroom.

Choosing the Right Book The right book depends on your child's reading level, of course. Ideally, you'd like reading materials that include only letter-sound combinations he already knows. As he learns new letter-sound combinations, the books he reads include those as well. This is another reason it pays to use a phonics program that teaches letter-sound pairings in order of frequency. There are book sets (e.g., *The Bob Books*) that respect this order, so your child sees only words that he ought to be able to read. Your best bet is to ask your child's teacher for recommendations because she knows how far your child has progressed.

Lots of children have a favorite book that they want to read again and again. Often it's one they have listened to so many times that they have memorized it, and so when they "read" it to you, you can tell they are pretty much reciting. It's not that they are dodging the harder work of decoding. Rather, they are enjoying a glimpse of what it's like to truly read, and that's a powerful motivator. So about half the time my youngest asked, I'd listen to her "read" *Go Dog, Go* (mercifully, the short version), and half

Figure 5.5. Reading practice is taxing. To maximize the chances that your child's attitude stays upbeat, try to pick a time for reading practice when he's least likely to be tired or hungry.
Source: © Ivanna Buldakova—Fotolia.com

the time I'd say, "Oh, I love that one too. But you read me that one yesterday. Let's pick another book today."

Shoot for at least one session each day, and make it brief—no more than five or ten minutes. That may not sound like much, but short bouts of practice can really pay off if they occur regularly. A little frustration during these sessions is normal, but if your child is having a bad day, just say something like, "That was great, but do you think maybe we're done?" (figure 5.5). Don't feel that you have to finish a book you've started. Of course, if he asks to keep reading, you should continue. But decoding is demanding when you are first learning, and the idea is that this process be fun. Finish the session by smiling and saying, "Thanks! I'm already looking forward to next time" or something similarly upbeat.

Providing Feedback   Feedback is an important part of any learning process, and that's what you're there for. At the same time, feedback can be distracting. So I suggest you talk as little as possible. The child needs to hear her own voice, not yours. You want to cheer her on and acknowledge when she's doing well—do that by smiling and nodding, not by saying, "Awesome!" or "Right!" For the same reason, don't initiate conversations about the story. That's just the opposite of what you do when you're reading aloud. Learning to decode is occupying all of your child's attention, and she can't think about two things at once. Switching back and forth between decoding and meaning is not going to help. But of course, you should (briefly) answer questions your child asks and acknowledge comments she makes.

If your child gets stuck on a word, don't be too quick to tell her what it is. (Likewise, when she's writing and asks how a word is spelled, she should make her best guess before you provide support.) And *don't* suggest that she guess what word makes sense. You're practicing decoding. In fact, most kids do a lot of guessing without your suggesting it because it's a strategy that has worked fairly well with very simple books. You're working toward the more general skill that will carry her through the complicated stuff. So when your child guesses, just smile and say, "Sound it out," even if she has guessed right.

Cover part of the word so all she can see is the part that's giving her trouble. If she's totally stumped, cover all but the initial letter (or two-letter combination, as appropriate). If she still needs help, remind her of the relevant rule: "Right. That letter usually says AW, but when there are two together, they say something else." The same strategies apply if your child reads a word incorrectly. Don't just blurt out a correction. Say "oops" or something else brief, and point to the missed word. See if she gets it. If not, offer support (figure 5.6).

Sometimes kids make a lot of mistakes because they try to read faster than they are really able. Other times they read excruciatingly slowly in an effort to avoid all mistakes. As in any other mental activity, speed and

mispelled

Figure 5.6. Don't be an auto-correct. Which way are you more likely to learn the correct spelling of "egregious": You notice that auto-correct fixes it for you, or you're told that the spelling is wrong and you try again to spell it correctly? When your child reads a word incorrectly, don't just say the word: let him take another try.
Source: © Daniel Willingham.

accuracy can be traded. There's no reason not to encourage your child to speed up or slow down a bit. Again, this can be done mostly with gentle gesture and minimal talking.

Dealing with Frustration   You'll note that I keep mentioning that you should smile, you should be upbeat, and so on. For me (and for many other parents I've spoken with), there were moments when listening to my kids read was the kind of sweet, parent-child activity I had imagined. And though I foresaw the moments that my child would be frustrated, I didn't foresee that *I* would be. My child would stop to comment on complete irrelevancies. I would suggest five times that she read faster, and she would ignore me. I would remind her of the sound "ou" makes, and she would forget *on the very next word.* There are going to be frustrating moments, but it's essential that you don't show that it's getting to you. If the interaction is negative, that emotion may rub off on reading, but even if it doesn't, it's going to make your child reluctant to partner with you for reading.

I can offer four suggestions if you find yourself frustrated. First, the habit of not talking much is not only good for your child (so she hears mostly her own voice, reading) but also good for maintaining your composure when you're frustrated. Second, when you do speak, you can usually find an intonation other than frustration that carries your message in a positive way. When my youngest would look to me for help on the same word three times in sixty seconds, my inclination was to shout, "You KNOW this one." I trained myself to say, "You know this one," with the intonation of, "You sly dog." I probably should have said nothing, but at least I used a positive tone. Third, remind yourself that the whole session is only five or ten minutes. Fourth, if you find that you just can't keep it together, quit. Ask your child to read with you later. Grinding through the process gives a little practice in decoding, but it carries too high a cost in motivation.

Teaching Your Child

You may wonder whether reading with your child for one or two brief sessions each day is enough. How about honest-to-goodness instruction, not just practice?

Let's start with the easy case. If you never thought about phonological awareness before reading this book and now realize that your six-year-old is not very good at hearing individual speech sounds, by all means, work on it. Phonological awareness exercises really are silly fun, and it's pretty hard to do them incorrectly, so play the games described in chapter 2, as well as any others that his teacher recommends.

What about decoding? Given that I emphasized the importance of phonics instruction earlier in this chapter, you might think I'd say, "*Someone* has to provide systematic phonics instruction, and if the teacher doesn't do it, you'll have to." But that's not what I'm going to say.

There are very few classrooms in the United States with no phonics instruction. First, teachers know the research literature and they know that phonics instruction is important. Second, many school districts (or states) mandate that kids take tests that tap their knowledge of phonics. Third, the reason I'm so strong on phonics is not that it's *impossible* to learn to read without it. It's that systematic phonics instruction maximizes the odds that everyone in the class will learn to read. Some kids—not many, but some—really do learn with very little instruction of any sort. Others learn with relatively modest support. So sure, if you have a choice, I would urge that your child be in a classroom that teaches phonics systematically. But you may not have that choice. What if phonics instruction seems kind of light? Then what?

I encourage you to be *very* cautious about providing reading instruction at home. There are studies showing that such teaching can help children learn to read, but in these studies, parents are trained in specific techniques by the researchers. If you're not trained by researchers (or your child's teacher), you're either going to go with your gut instincts about how to teach (which is dicey) or you'll choose one of the many products out there for parents to work on phonics with their kids. Many of these products are not sound in how they approach reading instruction, and most are terribly boring. As one reading specialist put it to me, "Phonics worksheets, disguised as computer apps and imposed by parents on their kids, are probably the number one destroyer of reading motivation." I see reading motivation as fragile and as difficult to bring back once it's gone. The proper role for a parent is enthusiastic cheerleader and good model of reading, not assigner of reading chores.

That said, if your child is really having trouble learning to decode—I mean *really* having trouble—then I completely reverse my advice. You need to be sure that your child is getting explicit phonics instruction. That, of course, raises the question of what constitutes good progress in learning to read.

When to Be Concerned

Some typical rules of thumb for an American kindergarten might be:

- By Halloween, know the letters.
- By Christmas, read some regular three-letter words.
- By spring break, read most three-letter words.
- By year's end, read some words with more complex blends.

But this rule of thumb really works only if it's consistent with what's being taught. As I was writing this chapter, I heard about a kindergarten classroom in which the teacher introduced four letters in the first nine weeks. That sounds like a pretty slow pace to me, but of course I don't know what else the kids were doing. I've said before I think that many American schools spend too much time on English language arts in the early elementary grades at the expense of nearly all other subjects. So if my child were in a classroom with a slow reading pace but with terrific math, science, history, music, and art, personally, I wouldn't complain.

· · · · · · · · · · · ·

As I've emphasized throughout this book, we need to attend to all three components of reading—decoding, comprehension, and motivation—at all ages. It's easy to forget about comprehension as kids are learning to decode, but it's vital that we don't. In the next chapter, we turn our attention to the continued building of knowledge during the early elementary years.

Keeping It Simple Summary

At School

- Systematic phonics instruction
- Children's literature
- Opportunities to write, speak, and listen, as well as read

At Home

- Have your child read to you, ideally every day, for brief (five- or ten-minute) sessions.
- Resist the urge to engage in reading instruction unless you have reason to believe you know what you're doing.
- Monitor that your child is making reasonable reading progress.

NOTES

"Hide from them all the ABCs.": Quoted in Manguel (1996, p. 79).

"'skeleton-shaped, bloodless, ghostly apparitions'": Mann (1841).

"still put forward today by some theorists": Goodman (1996).

"no more than fifty-five hundred years old": Robinson (2007).

"blue-ribbon panels of scientists": National Institute of Child Health and Human Development (2000); Rose (2006); EU High Level Group of Experts on Literacy (2012).

"US scientific organizations": National Research Council (1998); Rayner, Foorman, Perfetti, Pesetsky, and Seidenberg (2001).

"depending on what the child knows when reading instruction begins": Jeynes and Littell (2000); Sonnenschein, Stapleton, and Benson (2009); Stahl and Miller (1989).

"so was born 'balanced literacy'": Fountas and Pinnell (1996); Pressley (2002).

"a handbook for teachers published by the New York City Department of Education": Stabiner, Chasin, and Haver (2003).

"a lot of variation in what happened in their classrooms": Bingham and Hall-Kenyon (2013).

"different kids learn better from different activities": Connor, Morrison, and Katch (2004); Connor, Morrison, and Petrella (2004).

"most early elementary teachers are using some version of balanced literacy": Xue and Meisels (2004).

"allot scant time to phonics instruction": Rayner, Pollatsek, Ashby, and Clifton (2012).

"other research that kids (and adults) can't focus on two things at a time": Pashler (1999).

"technology has a modest positive effect on reading outcomes": Cheung and Slavin (2011).

"the modest effect is actually typical for educational technology interventions": Hattie (2009); Tamim, Bernard, Borokhovski, Abrami, and Schmid (2011).

"the student's relationship with the teacher, a factor known to be important in early reading": Mashburn et al. (2008).

"There are studies showing that such teaching can help children learn to read": Senechal and Young (2008).

6

BANKING KNOWLEDGE
FOR THE FUTURE

When a child is learning to decode, we obviously expect little by way of reading comprehension. But by grade 3 or so, we start to expect that students can comprehend longer, more complex texts and that they will branch out into reading texts from genres other than stories. At home and at school, they may be exposed to letters, newspaper articles, and expository text like encyclopedia entries. Kids are still not asked to work with the texts in a serious way (e.g., to use them in research)—that won't come until the upper elementary years. But once children can decode reliably, the expectations for comprehension begin to increase.

UNDERSTANDING LONGER TEXTS

We begin by considering what's required to understand longer texts. This entails not just connecting sentences, as I discussed in chapter 1, but the way that readers connect many ideas into something bigger. After that, we'll consider how schools can support the development of this more challenging comprehension task.

Capturing Big Ideas

Reading comprehension begins when the reader extracts ideas from the sentences he reads. Then he connects ideas that are about the same thing ("The tissues are on the desk. The tissues are white.") or ideas that are causally related ("The stranger tapped on the window. The dog barked."). The result of making these connections is a network of related ideas, analogous to a social network. Imagine a web of connections that vary in strength.

That's a good start at explaining reading comprehension, but it's not enough. Consider this text:

> Sally decided to go to the big market downtown. The downtown area had recently been renovated. The market included a large deli. The deli man really liked capicola ham. The deli man's wife wants a new car but she can't decide what type to get. The bank where she applied for a loan has gold carpeting.

If understanding were merely a matter of connecting ideas into a network—about-the-same-thing connections and causal connections—this passage would not seem strange. But it does, and it's not hard to describe why. There's no big picture. Each idea can be connected to another, but there's no *overall* idea of what the paragraph is about.

Somehow readers need to represent in memory the big picture of what they read. One of the seminal experiments on how readers meet this challenge used very brief text similar to this one: "Two birds sat on a branch. An open birdcage sat on the ground beneath them." Now suppose I asked you, "Was the branch above the birdcage?" If you had nothing but the specific sentences in your memory, you could answer that question by combining what you were told with some logical inferences, like this:

> I was told the birds are above the branch.
> Therefore, the branch is below the birds.
> I was told the birdcage is beneath the birds, on the ground.
> By transitive inference, the birdcage must be below the branch.
> Therefore, the branch must be above the birdcage.

Our intuition tells us that we don't answer the question that way, and research supports that intuition. But what choice is there but to answer the question based on what you read?

The alternative is that you create a representation of the whole situation the sentences describe. It's called, appropriately enough, the *situation*

Figure 6.1. Nonverbal situation model. Visual mental images are a way to represent complex relationships without being tied to one description. You could consult this mental image and just as easily verify "birdcage is under branch" or "branch is over birdcage" however their positions were described in what you read.
Source: © Matthew Cole—Fotolia.com.

model. A situation model helps you keep track of many related ideas (e.g., the relative positions of the birds, branch, and birdcage) independent of the particular sentences used to describe those ideas. The situation model could be verbal, but it doesn't have to be (figure 6.1).

Background Knowledge Revisited

You'll recall that background knowledge was needed to make the causal connections among sentences. The same is true of the situation model. Background knowledge both influences your ability to create the situation model in the first place and colors your understanding of a text's overall message. And as was true for the background knowledge that allows you to connect sentences, writers omit information needed to create the situation model on the assumption that readers already know it. For example, have a look at this text:

It's possible to use an analog watch as a compass! Simply hold the watch in your hand and rotate it so that the hour hand points at the sun. Find the location halfway between the hour hand and twelve o'clock—that's south. (If you live in the Southern Hemisphere, it's north.)

Some knowledge is required to interpret individual sentences and connect them (e.g., the meaning of "hour hand"), and the writer doesn't bother to provide that knowledge. But even if you have all of the knowledge required to connect the sentences, your situation model would include other facts from your background knowledge like these:

- That it's unusual to use a tool designed for one purpose for an altogether different purpose
- Why you might need a compass in a situation where you don't have one
- That ad hoc tools like this are often pretty rough in serving their function, but if you're lost, rough information about direction is much better than none at all

That background information highlights the big picture for you. It's vital to appreciating what makes this text useful and interesting. Now consider this parallel text:

It's possible to know where parts of the brain are simply by looking at the skull. The skulls of mammals have three large plates that meet at the top of the head. That's called the *bregma point*. There are brain atlases that describe the location of different parts of the brain relative to the bregma point.

Although this passage, like the previous one, describes how to find something, I'm guessing that reading it felt different. It's not that you don't understand it. The sentences make sense, and how they relate to one another makes sense. What's missing is some sense of deeper understanding. That's because a well-developed situation model would have other information from your background knowledge. You probably don't know why you'd want to know where parts of the brain are simply by looking at the skull. And while you might guess that this method of localization is imperfect (just like the watch-compass technique), it's harder to judge whether this rough information would really be better than none at all.

It's hard to appreciate just what a difference background knowledge makes to your situation model and thus to the experience of reading comprehension, so here's one more example:

Carol Harris was a problem child from birth. She was wild, stubborn, and violent. By the time Carol turned eight, she was still unmanageable. Her parents were very concerned about her mental health. There was no good institution for her problem in her state. Her parents finally decided to take some action. They hired a private teacher for Carol.

I'm wagering that you had little trouble reading this paragraph with good comprehension. But suppose I had told you, "By the way, the character, Carol Harris? That's actually Helen Keller. They just changed her name for the story." That alters your understanding. For example, you interpret statements about her wildness and violence in light of what you know about Helen Keller's blindness and deafness, and the frustration and despair it might have caused.

Imagine a person reading this paragraph without knowing anything about Helen Keller. This reader would "comprehend" it as you did when the name Carol Harris was used. All the sentences make sense, and the paragraph as a whole hangs together. And yet an important aspect of meaning is absent. Even if you have sufficient knowledge to connect the sentences, there is usually a still deeper level of comprehension that can be reached. That's the situation model: you integrate the ideas in the text not just into an overall big picture; that big picture is colored by other relevant knowledge from your memory.

WHAT'S HAPPENING AT SCHOOL

Although the demands for comprehension are modest in kindergarten and first grade (because the focus is on learning to decode), they increase rapidly thereafter. As I've emphasized, background knowledge is vital to support comprehension, so children should be acquiring knowledge during those early elementary years. But there are obstacles to this learning.

Slowly Increasing Demands on Comprehension

Developing the situation model becomes increasingly important as kids move through the elementary years, for two reasons. First, texts become more complex, meaning we place greater expectations on children to coordinate meanings from the beginning to the end. For example in the Common Core State Standards, the recommended texts for first graders include books like *Little Bear* and *Frog and Toad Together*, and others that feature large illustrations on each page with modest amounts of text. But the second- and third-grade band of texts includes *Charlotte's Web* and *Sarah, Plain and Tall*—much longer, much more involved texts. The reader must create larger chunks of meaning, and so the situation model will be more complicated.

Students must also coordinate meanings over multiple texts; they apply knowledge from prior texts when they read something new. Suppose a child is passionate about butterflies. He reads books about their behavior, he has identification guides, and so on. The situation model of each text doesn't lie in memory, totally insulated from the situation model of other texts. What he knows from these different sources ought to get brewed together. As kids move through school, we increasingly expect that they will remember and apply things they have learned before to new reading.

Second, students start to encounter a greater variety of genres. At the start of school, most of the texts children read or hear are stories. Thus, most kids come to understand typical Western narrative structure

Figure 6.2. Learning new genres. "Literacy" means stories until the early elementary years. At that point children start to encounter new genres. Teachers might have kids publish their own newspaper as a writing project, or they may encourage children to read age-appropriate news stories on one of the many websites designed for kids. "Here, There, Everywhere" was created by a former *Today Show* producer who wanted to bring the news to young children.

Source: © Alexandra Thiessen. Here, There, Everywhere website screen shot reproduced by permission.

pretty well: there is a main character who has a goal, there is an obstacle preventing the character from reaching the goal, the character has some adventures and complications in pursuing the goal, and then at the end of the story, the character reaches the goal. Knowing that basic structure helps the child's comprehension. As she reads, each new character and event she encounters can be fit into that familiar story structure. When children begin to read other genres of text, however, they no longer have that support to comprehension; they must learn the conventions of other genres (figure 6.2).

A number of studies in the past thirty years show that knowledge of specific topics is a powerful aid to comprehension. In one, elementary school children took standardized tests of their verbal comprehension and reasoning skills. They were also tested on their knowledge of soccer. The experimenters separated the students into four groups based on their soccer knowledge (high or low) and their general verbal skills (high or low). Then students read a story about soccer, and experimenters measured their comprehension and recall (figure 6.3).

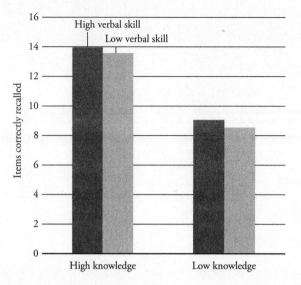

Figure 6.3. Knowledge and verbal skill. The graph shows how much readers remembered of a text about soccer. Kids identified as having "high verbal skills" remembered a bit more than kids with "low verbal skills" (compare the dark and light bars). But that effect is tiny compared to the effect of knowledge of soccer.

Source: "Domain specific knowledge and memory performance: A comparison of high- and low-aptitude children" by W. Schneider, J. Körkel, & F. E. Weinert, in *Journal of Educational Psychology, 81*, 306–312. Data are from Table 2, p. 309. © American Psychological Association, 1989.

In this experiment, "verbal skill" doesn't mean much compared to knowledge. Knowing the kinds of things that generally happen in a soccer game and the sequence in which they are likely to happen provides the same sort of framework that knowledge of stories would.

Here we see still another reason to ensure that students have broad background knowledge if our goal is that they be able to read most any text written for the layperson. Knowledge is important not just for connecting sentences; it makes a separate contribution to understanding longer, more challenging texts. How can we ensure that kids learn what they need to know in the early elementary years?

The Importance of Acquiring Background Knowledge

Research shows that reading depends on broad knowledge of all subjects: history, civics, science, mathematics, literature, drama, music, and so on.

Figure 6.4. First European colonists. Typically children learn about the arrival of the first European colonists (here depicted on a panel from the US Capitol Rotunda) in their early elementary years But wouldn't it be easier to appreciate the arrival of the colonists if you first studied the Native Americans who were already here? And wouldn't it be easier to understand their lives and culture if you had already had a unit about farming? And wouldn't it be easier to understand farming if you had first studied plants?
Source: http://commons.wikimedia.org/wiki/File:Flickr_-_USCapitol_-_Landing_of_the_Pilgrims,_1620.jpg.

Furthermore, it makes sense that subject matter knowledge be sequenced. It's commonly appreciated that mathematical concepts build on one another, and they are easier to learn if they are sequenced properly. The same is true of other subjects. It's easier to understand why the last remnants of European colonialism crumbled in the 1950s if you know something about World War II. It's easier to understand World War II if you know something about the Great Depression. And so on. So the content that students will learn in the earliest grades is hugely important. It's the bedrock of everything that is to come (figure 6.4).

Still, talk of "academic content" in early grades makes some adults anxious. So let me address some of the more common concerns.

Can't Kids Just Be Kids? When people hear "academic content in pre-kindergarten," they sometimes jump to the conclusion that it means studying long lists of facts and that the mode of teaching will be a lot of teacher talk, followed by practice worksheets, followed by tests. After all, that's how older kids are often taught academic content. But if you've read this far, you know that drilling and testing are not my style. I'm thinking of activities like read-alouds, projects, independent work with materials, field trips, video, and, yes, listening to the teacher, visitors, and one another.

Ideally, when kids get a bit older, they learn rich content as they practice reading. Unfortunately, that's not likely, as the commonly available basal readers tend not to be heavy on ideas and tend not to have a systematic sequence to whatever ideas they do contain. So schools and districts need to pay special attention to the need for knowledge. They won't get it from most off-the-shelf products.

Is This Developmentally Appropriate?   Another take on the "can't kids just be kids" argument is to suggest that kindergarten children *cannot* learn certain concepts. The usual term is that such content is "developmentally inappropriate." In other words, there is a predictable sequence to the development of the mind, and six-year-olds are cognitively incapable of understanding certain concepts. This concern was voiced strongly in 2013 when New York State posted part of a first-grade curriculum module on early civilizations that included vocabulary terms like "sarcophagus" and "cuneiform."

A number of bloggers took to the web, suggesting that such a lesson would be developmentally inappropriate. How can children be expected to understand anything about a five-thousand-year-old Mesopotamian civilization when they (1) have no concept of five thousand years; (2) have no concept of where countries are located on a globe (e.g., "modern-day Iraq" will be meaningless to them), and (3) don't know what their own civilization is, much less someone else's?

My reply will necessarily be brief, but here goes. Drawing broad conclusions about what children can and can't understand doesn't work because their understanding depends on the task. I've heard people say "six-year-olds can't understand abstractions." But learning to use the word "dog" (or any other category label) is an abstraction. The idea that "dog" applies not just to particular objects but to any instance of a class of objects (many of which look dissimilar) is an abstraction. Whether a particular abstraction can be learned depends more on what the child already knows and less on some biologically predetermined course of development, linked to the child's age (figure 6.5).

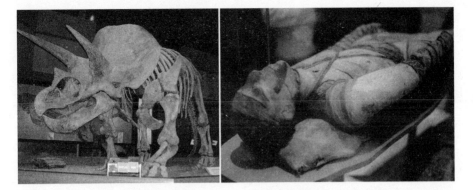

Figure 6.5. Old, dead subjects. The idea that children will be baffled and bored learning about things that are unfamiliar and cannot be physically encountered seems belied by the fascination many children have for dinosaurs and ancient Egypt.
Source: Dinosaur © Redvodka; derivative work, original by Mathnight, via Flickr: http://commons.wikimedia .org/wiki/Dinosaur#mediaviewer/File:TriceratopsTyrrellMuseum1.jpg. Mummy © Klafubra, via Flickr: http:// commons.wikimedia.org/wiki/Mummy#mediaviewer/File:Mummy_at_British_Museum.jpg.

"Developmental appropriateness" rests on an assumption about the mind that is probably wrong. It suggests that the mind develops in discrete stages, where one month the child's mind works one way and then a few months later it works another way. That's the idea behind "they are incapable of learning that, but in a year most will be ready." It's more accurate to describe the learning of new ideas as coming in fits and starts; the child understands in one situation but not another. The child shows understanding on Tuesday and then doesn't in the identical situation on Thursday. So it will be with children gaining some appreciation of what it means for a civilization to have existed five thousand years ago. If you wait until you're certain they can understand it, you will wait too long. And you will find that students from wealthy homes are more likely to have been exposed to ideas that help them understand it earlier.

I can't resist providing one example from the classroom of my wife, an early elementary teacher. She teaches seven-year-olds about the creation of the universe and the origins of humankind. She reads a description of the big bang; the subsequent formation of galaxies, stars, and planets; the formation of the earth; the coming of life; the development of other species; and finally the development of humans. (The description is about three pages long.) As she's reading, an assistant unrolls a strip of black felt. It's a foot wide and forty-five feet long. The last sentence describes humankind emerging, and that's when the last of the felt is exposed—and it's covered by a thin red ribbon. The black felt represents the time since the big bang, and the red ribbon is the amount of time that humankind has existed. So after seeing that, do seven-year-olds have a perfect conceptual understanding of vast time? Of course not. But they are closer than they were.

Making Time

A more serious concern is time. I'm suggesting that more attention be paid to content knowledge, and attention means time. There's less instructional time in early elementary classrooms because students take longer to transition from one activity to another. And once a teacher has done some phonics work, some read-alouds, and some writing, how much time is left in the day? Well, in a couple of studies from the early 2000s, researchers observed several hundred first- and third-grade classrooms across the United States and wrote down what happened (figure 6.6).

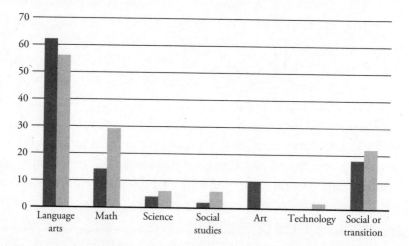

Figure 6.6. Time in classrooms. Time spent on different subjects in first grade (darker bars) and third grade (lighter bars). The numbers add to greater than 100 percent because some lessons combined more than one subject.

Source: First-grade data from "The relation of global first-grade classroom environment to structural classroom features and teacher and student behaviors" by the National Institute of Child Health and Human Development, & Early Child Care Research Network. *Elementary School Journal, 102,* 367–387. Data from Table 2, p. 376. © The University of Chicago Press, 2002. Third-grade data from "A day in third grade: A large-scale study of classroom quality and teacher and student behavior" by the National Institute of Child Health and Human Development, & Early Child Care Research Network. *Elementary School Journal, 105,* 305–323. Data from Table 2, p. 314. © The University of Chicago Press, 2005.

As you can see, language arts and math account for nearly all instructional time. Science and social studies are neglected.* So in answer to the objection that "there's no time to add content," I answer, "We have to make time." And it's pretty obvious what to cut, at least looking at these averages. We have to curtail language arts activities that we think offer students the least benefit and replace them with science, history, drama, civics, and so on. If we don't, we can expect a cost to reading comprehension in later grades.

WHAT TO DO AT HOME

The last section ended with a pretty sobering set of statistics about time spent on content knowledge in schools. In chapter 5, I encouraged you to count on your child's teacher to get him reading, but when it comes to knowledge building, you can't exhort the schools and hope for the best. This work will fall to you. In chapter 3, I described desirable practices meant to spark interest in knowledge—those are still desirable. But as kids get older, some of the activities take a different shape.

Talking

You still want to ask your child questions, of course, but as they grow, you can expect them to provide longer answers and you can pose more open-ended questions. The most natural thing to ask about is what happened at school. You'll get social stuff in response—what happened at recess or at lunch. That's fine, but it's nice to know about the rest of the day (which also gives you the chance to express interest in what he learned—not just because he's the one learning it, but because you find the topic itself interesting). "What else happened?" will likely draw a blank look. The best strategy is to pose a more specific question. For example, if you know that the class writes in response to a teacher-generated prompt for five minutes each day, ask, "What was the writing prompt today?" So that means it pays to

---

*These data are unfortunately a bit old now; they were collected in 1997–1999 (first grade) and 1999–2001 (third grade). But I don't know many teachers or administrators who think that No Child Left Behind has decreased the emphasis on reading and math, and recent smaller-scale studies support this general conclusion.

know something about the specifics of what's happening in the classroom, information you might glean from a classroom newsletter or website or from back-to-school night. Or, better, talk to the teacher about it.

I think children learn a couple of things from telling you about their day. They get practice in telling a story, in putting their thoughts together and relating what happened in a way that has a beginning, middle, and end. So even if the playground drama of first-grade alliances is not what you meant when you asked what happened at school, bear in mind that your child is getting some benefit from telling you this story. And she'll get even more if you pay attention, ask questions, and feign confusion if she's not telling the story in a logical sequence.

In addition to providing feedback about your child's storytelling, show him how it's done. Tell your own stories. This is a marvelous age at which children understand that you were once young, and they generally find it fascinating to hear about your life. Hearing your stories provides a model, and there is often more background information in them than you would think. My father told me countless stories about his boyhood in Rome, Georgia, in the 1930s—stories about games of capture the flag in the alleyways among downtown buildings; stories of lying, sleepless, on sweat-soaked sheets on July nights, waiting for the brief, relieving breeze brought by the oscillating fan; and the story that became the town sensation one summer: a teen dared a soda jerk holding a butcher knife to chop off his finger, certain that the soda jerk would chicken out, whereupon the soda jerk, certain that the teen would pull his hand away at the last moment, chopped off the finger. In addition to bringing me closer to my father and learning something about how to weave a good narrative, those stories taught me what alleyways, oscillating fans, and soda jerks are.

Reading

Naturally you should continue reading to your child. Don't quit because your child can read or because your child now reads to you. Remember, when he was little, you read to you him not because he couldn't do it himself but because it was a pleasurable way to spend time together. That hasn't changed. And given that learning to decode inevitably entails some struggle, read-alouds are the time to remind him that reading brings joy. Then, too, as your child grows in ability to follow and appreciate more complex narrative, there's a greater chance to introduce books that you enjoy.

In chapter 3 I suggested that read-alouds for young children could include nonfiction. Some children immediately take to fact-filled books—one seven-year-old told me in a grave voice, "I like books with information"—but others don't. This is a good age to give nonfiction another try, because your child has probably developed some personal interest that can guide your selection of a nonfiction book: soccer, bugs, ballet, whatever. There are terrific books that are still loaded with pictures like those targeted to younger kids, but with richer text.

Certain topics dominate nonfiction at this age: animals, weather, historical subjects. Another idea is to try a picture-rich book related to a game that your child loves, even if the text is beyond her. If she loves Barbie, why not a book on the history of Barbie fashions? If your child loves gross-out toys, how about Nick Arnold's *Disgusting Digestion*? The Hexbug enthusiast might enjoy the *Eyewitness: Robots* book. If you're at the library and these ideas elicit little interest from your child, get a book on the subject that your child hasn't yet seen and drop it in his bathroom book basket without mentioning it. You never know. (Or if your kids are like mine, pretend the book is yours and leave it in *your* bathroom book basket, which will make it more attractive.)

Playing

On the subject of games, some board games are useful sources of background knowledge. I'm not talking about "games" that are really drill sessions in phonics or number facts dressed up to look like games. These merit the disdainful descriptor "chocolate-covered broccoli." But some games are genuine fun *and* require knowledge as part of their play: *The Scrambled States of America* for US geography, for example, *Apples to Apples Junior* for vocabulary, and *Scrabble Junior* for spelling. I especially like games that don't demand knowledge to play, but expose kids to it incidentally. *Zeus on the Loose* uses Greek gods as characters. In *Masterpiece* the point is to collect valuable art, and the works depicted are classics of the Western canon. *20th Century Time Travel* is a rummy-like card game, with history facts on the cards, not unlike the classic card game *Authors*. You do have to exercise some caution, as many games claim to be educational. If there are dice, then it's a counting game. If it requires sorting, then kids are finding patterns.

Home-grown word games can still be good fun, but are likely to change as kids get older. They've probably outgrown phonological awareness rhyme games, but now know enough words for vocabulary games. My kids like to keep it simple: I say a word and they are to guess the synonym I am thinking of. Remember the old game show *Password*? That's basically it. Sometimes they give the clue and I guess, but the other arrangement is easier for them; words that are hard to bring to mind are easily recognized when someone else says them. More challenging is the two-word version. I think of two words that rhyme, and then provide a descriptive phrase, for example, "What do you call it when your trousers do the waltz?" A pants dance.

My wife plays another version of the synonym game with the kids in her class that they have dubbed "Say It Again, Sam." It can be played by kids of varying ages. Someone starts by saying any sentence, for example, "This cupcake has pink frosting." Each player then rephrases the original sentence. A five-year-old might say, "This small cake has pink frosting." A ten-year-old might be more ambitious in trying to avoid repetition of the original and say, "The small cake before me is covered in a mixture of sugar and butter that looks light red." Kids can get surprisingly creative (and surprisingly funny) when they get absorbed in this game.

Gaining Independence

As your child learns to decode and gains fluency and confidence, you'll want to start teaching her to do on her own things that you have, until now, done for her. Indeed, she'll want to do those things herself. When a word needs a sharper definition or a fact is in dispute, you have made a habit of finding the needed information in a dictionary or encyclopedia. Now is a good time to buy your child her own kid-friendly reference books. But remember, it's not obvious to the neophyte how to use these books. She'll need your guidance.

These fledgling research skills can also be practiced when you plan a family trip. Going to Disneyworld? Let's get out the globe and find Orlando. How can we find out what the weather will be like so we can pack the right clothing? Why is it so warm in Orlando if it's so cold here? And so on. Even if you're taking just a day trip, find your destination on a map and read up a bit about where you're going (figure 6.7).

Another sure sign of your child's independence: she's ready for her own magazine subscription. That offers a triple thrill: (1) there are a lot of terrific magazines for kids, (2) having her own subscription is a sign of being more grown up, and (3) everybody loves getting mail. Check out *Ladybug, Click, Highlights, National Geographic Kids, Ranger Rick* (and *Ranger Rick, Jr.*), *Kind News* (primary), *Mocomi, Your Big Backyard, New*

Figure 6.7. Buy a globe. Globes seem old-fashioned in the age of the web, and they are not cheap—a decent one will set you back fifty dollars or more. But I think they are a good investment. There is no substitute for a globe to give your child a sense of geographic distance. And your child will make surprising discoveries (the United States isn't bigger? Lichtenstein is a country?) for years.
Source: © Christian Fischer—Fotolia.

Moon, Our Little Earth, Nickelodeon, Sports Illustrated Kids, American Girl, Stone Soup, and *Time for Kids*.

Magazines not only build knowledge, they will, we hope, keep kids motivated to read. In the next chapter we'll consider other measures to maintain the motivation of early elementary readers.

Keeping It Simple Summary

At School

- Substantive learning in science, geography, history, drama, civics, music, and art becomes part of school.

At Home

- Keep doing what you've been doing, but with changes that reflect your child's increasing maturity and independence.
- Tell stories to and elicit stories from your child.
- Consider a greater proportion of nonfiction in your read-alouds and choices for your child's reading.

NOTES

" 'Two birds sat on a branch. An open birdcage sat beneath them.' ": Barclay, Bransford, Franks, McCarrell, and Nitsch (1974).

The Carol Harris story is from Sulin and Dooling (1974).

"tend not to be heavy on ideas": Duke (2000); Moss (2008); Pentimonti, Zucker, Justice, and Kaderavek (2010).

"My reply will necessarily be brief, but here goes.": For a review, see Willingham (2008).

"a couple of studies from the early 2000s": National Institute of Child Health and Human Development. Early Child Care Research Network (2002, 2005).

"and recent smaller-scale studies support this general conclusion": Baniflower et al. (2013); Claessens, Engel, and Curran (2013).

7

Preventing a Motivation Backslide

In the introduction, I cited a depressing statistic: although the average child's attitude toward reading is positive in early elementary school, it gets more negative year by year. By puberty, the typical kid is indifferent toward reading or even feels a bit negative. The early elementary years, when children are still mostly positive about reading, is the time to think about how to prevent this decline.

What's Happening at School

In the early elementary years, children begin to read themselves, not just to listen to others read to them. In addition, they have a classroom of other kids to whom they might compare their reading achievement. These constitute new contributors to reading self-concept and reading attitudes.

Self-Concept

Young children (say, age four or five) tend to see themselves as good at everything; they are smart, strong, and accomplished, and they are usually eager to offer evidence, such as their ability to swing really high and sing the ABC song (whether or not they actually know the whole thing). At the same time, their self-concept tends to be very concrete: being smart, for example, means being able to sing the ABC song.

As kids get older, say age seven or eight, self-concepts become increasingly abstract. Being "smart" is not just a matter of one or another accomplishment; kids understand "smart" as something that integrates many

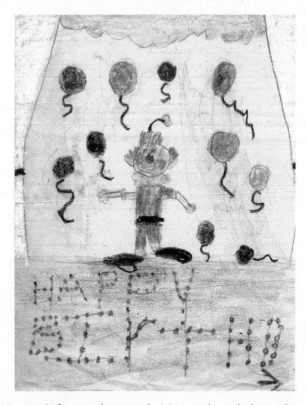

Figure 7.1. My sister's first-grade artwork. My sister brought home drawings from first grade, and my mother thought she was a prodigy. My sister, comparing her work to her classmates, insisted it was nothing special. My mother thought she was being modest, but after attending back-to-school night (and seeing the drawings that other kids had done), my mother reported to my father, "She was right."
Source: © Sherry Lotan.

behaviors. They begin to splice diverse experiences into a narrative that describes who they are. And by this age, self-concept is no longer a frenzy of self-congratulation. Kids begin to understand that they have some positive qualities but lack others. They come to this understanding through comparison. They see that although they thought they were fast and strong, other kids can swing higher and run faster than they can (figure 7.1).

Reading Self-Concept   Small children get their sense of themselves as readers from their understanding that reading is a family value and also from being read to and enjoying it. Whether they are a good reader does not contribute to their self-concept—they aren't reading by themselves yet, and their self-assessments would, in any event, not be very realistic.

But in the early elementary years, kids compare their reading progress with others in the class, and that will contribute to their reading self-concept, for better or worse. These comparisons are often made easier because teachers group children of similar reading accomplishment so that they can read texts of similar difficulty. Teachers won't call them "smarties" and "dullards," but even first graders won't miss that everybody in the "bluebirds" group decodes better than everybody in the "robins" group.

It's no small matter to keep up the motivation and self-image of kids who can plainly perceive that their reading isn't going well. The best recipe seems to be equal parts of celebration of individual children's success, along with emotional support: acknowledgment that it's a tough thing that he's learning, coupled with full confidence that he can do it.

Curriculum as a Self-Concept Amplifier   As someone who came to educational research later in my career, I'm sometimes asked what surprised me most about schooling when I started researching it. What struck me was the difference in the attitudes of students in kindergarten and students in fourth grade. (I'm not talking about research here, but about my observations in classrooms.) Kindergarten students, almost without exception, are happy to be there. Naturally they get bored or frustrated with this or that activity, but they are always game for whatever comes next. Not so fourth graders. After ten minutes in most fourth-grade classrooms, it's obvious to me which students do not view school as a place of opportunity and excitement but instead as a place where they fail and feel shame. When I've mentioned this observation to early elementary teachers, they often say, "You see it in fourth graders. We see it in second and even first graders." I am sure they are right.

I think there is a tie to literacy. Consider a child who finds learning to decode difficult. It's not lost on him that he struggles in a way that his classmates do not. Naturally this child will be dejected about reading, but consider that most of the time students spend in school is devoted to English language arts. If a student has a terrible time with reading, why *wouldn't* he conclude that school is just not for him? In chapter 6, I suggested that broadening the curriculum is crucial to build general knowledge, but making more space for other subjects in kindergarten may also pay off in motivation. The child who is struggling with reading may still dread it, but he knows that science is coming later, or history, or drama, and so his academic self-image stays more positive.

Attitudes

If children start school with positive reading attitudes but these attitudes slip year by year, then we want to be darn sure we know everything we can about what factors could be leading to the slide. There has been substantial research on the two classroom factors that seem most likely to have an impact: the type of instruction the child experiences and the teacher.

Instruction and Motivation   Phonics instruction seems really boring. It's rote memorization, devoid of meaning, and thus seems bound to make kids think reading is dull work. But research doesn't support that reasonable supposition. The particular way kids are taught to decode—phonics or whole-word instruction—doesn't affect attitudes. It may be that when kids are starting out, even reading disconnected words is somewhat rewarding. They might be excited to engage in this activity that they associate with older kids and grown-ups. It also may be that the materials used for whole-word instruction are not that exciting either (figure 7.2).

I don't know of data that directly support this explanation, but some research findings are consistent with it. I said that attitudes toward reading become more negative as kids get older. Well, that happens faster for kids who have a hard time learning to read. And making kids aware that they are having a hard time (by, for example, putting them in the "slow" reading group) makes the problem still worse. So there's some support for the commonsense idea that success in reading brings good reading attitudes.

Also, we should remember that when we compare whole-word and phonics methods, we're comparing just one part of a broader literacy program. For example, we would also predict that including good children's literature in a reading program would be associated with more positive attitudes, as would reading aloud to students. Both are true, and the data are copious and clear. So it may be that phonics is not all that much fun, but

The kitten is black.
Alice likes her kitten.
She gave it some milk.
The kitten likes milk.
Alice likes milk, too.
The kitten said, "Mew, mew!"
It went to sleep.

JANE L. HOXIE.

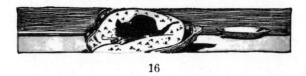

16

Figure 7.2. Whole-word reader. This page is taken from a book meant to be used with whole-word instruction. Even if your intent is that children plunge into exciting stories, they can't recognize enough words to construct a gripping tale when they are just learning to read.
Source: From The Elson Readers, Primer (Scott, Foresman, 1920).

the cost to motivation is modest and is hard to detect among the other aspects of the literacy program, all of which affect motivation.

The Impact of the Teacher on Reading Attitudes There's another (probably better) explanation for why the particular method of instruction doesn't affect student attitudes: what really matters is how the teacher implements the reading program. Studies going back to the 1960s have shown that student engagement is driven primarily by the teacher's actions, not the program. So what does a teacher do to make students enthusiastic about reading?

She offers support at the right time to the right student in the right amount. She sets a positive emotional tone for the classroom through her enthusiasm and confidence in her students. She shows emotional sensitivity, comforting students when things go badly and at the same time expressing confidence that they can be successful. She understands how to maintain the momentum of the lesson: when to switch activities if the class is draggy, when to end a lesson if the class has had enough, and when the students can be pushed a little harder. She knows who to call on to take a leadership role on a given day. She knows how to adjust the difficulty of the lesson on the fly so that it is challenging but not overwhelming. When you start listing the skills that are involved in executing a reading lesson, you see why the teacher makes such a difference.

The truth is that if you visit your child's classroom, it may not be obvious to you how skilled the teacher is. Look again at the previous paragraph and note the extent to which teachers must make decisions in the moment; they need to read their class (or an individual child) and *act*. Researchers estimate that teachers may make as many as one thousand decisions every school day. These moments are so evanescent, however, that it takes a very experienced eye to evaluate them. So what should you look for when you visit your child's class?

Features of Great Classrooms

Reading is given a place of prominence in effective classrooms, and by that I mean physical prominence. There's a classroom library, ideally one with a substantial collection. There are materials on the walls that are there for students to read—not just colorful posters or inspirational messages, but actual tools they will use again and again. For example, in one classroom I visited, I saw a large cartoon man, meant to help first graders make sure that their sentences were complete when they wrote: the head represented a capital letter at the start, and the feet, a punctuation mark. Other body parts represented nouns and verbs. Figure 7.3 shows another example of an effective poster.

Second, research shows that it's helpful when teachers model enthusiasm for reading and show children the benefits of reading. It is exciting to see the eyes of my child's teacher light up when she

Figure 7.3. A "word graveyard." Each construction paper "tombstone" shows a word that students had decided was too boring to be included in their writing anymore. If they were tempted to use one of these, they had to find a synonym.
Source: © Daniel Willingham.

discusses books. Effective reading teachers mention incidents from their daily lives that show that they read for pleasure—commenting on something from the newspaper, for example, or describing how a book affected them.

Great reading teachers create opportunities for students to see themselves as successful readers. This one is a little harder to spot. What you *don't* want to see is endless praise, especially praise that focuses on performance. If you praise performance (e.g., how quickly the child reads, or how accurately) then the child will, predictably enough, focus on performance.

Praising performance can result in children working to avoid failure, but you'd rather that failure be normalized. Children should view failure as an opportunity to learn something.

Instead of performance, you want your child to focus on learning. Research shows that kids are better motivated when teachers praise effort and praise children who are making choices to maximize their learning by, for example, selecting a book that is a bit challenging for them. When children get discouraged, the effective practice is to remind them that they've encountered obstacles before and surmounted them. The overarching principle is the same for parents and teachers: high expectations, along with confidence that the child can meet them, and the promise of support along the way. Classrooms that boost reading motivation offer opportunities for student choice. The purpose of choice is, as you'd expect, for students to feel greater ownership of and commitment to their reading. Teachers might let students decide where to read, or what to read (from a teacher-generated set of choices—a classroom library is a big help here), or perhaps how they will respond to the text (writing a report, conferencing with the teacher, and so on). Choice *can* go wrong, of course (e.g., if the student is allowed to choose a book with inappropriate content), but teachers are almost invariably sensitive to this danger.

WHAT TO DO AT HOME

It's easy to forget about reading motivation at home in the early elementary years. There are so many new activities your child might take on—piano lessons, perhaps, or an organized sport. And school is slowly becoming more academic and requires more attention. Reading can get crowded out, especially because you figure that your child is reading at school, and your child probably likes to read when he does so. But there's still a lot to do at home.

Keep It Up

Keep doing what you've been doing. It's still important to your child's motivation that she sees her parents and siblings reading, that there are books in the home, and so forth. If you just picked up this book and are alarmed because you have never done for your six-year-old all the stuff that I mentioned in previous chapters (e.g., reading aloud, asking questions), don't worry; it's not too late. There is evidence showing that starting when your child is in early elementary school is still a good idea.

How Parents Can Shape Reading Self-Concept

I've mentioned that at this age, children begin to compare themselves to others and that is an important determinant of self-image. Thus, self-image is not fixed. Kids change their minds about who they are as they make fresh comparisons either because their own behavior changes, their peer's behavior changes, or they choose new people as the basis of the comparison. So if your child has a negative reading self-image, don't give up.

Equally important, how the child thinks about his experiences counts more than the experiences themselves. Parents can guide the formation of that interpretation. For example, suppose a second grader tells his dad, "I'm no good at reading." Our instinct as parents is to make the child feel better and to protect his reading self-esteem. The shortest route seems to be denial: "Did your teacher say you're a bad reader? No? See, you're doing fine." A denial (with evidence) makes sense if the child really is doing well. But if he's not, denial is not going to work—not for an eight-year-old. Instead, his father might give him another interpretation of what's happened: "It's true, reading has been tough. I think that's because you've been spending so much time helping mom and me take care of your little brothers. I bet the other kids in your class have more chances to practice reading. Maybe we should do that." The child was ready to conclude, "I'm not a reader," but his father offers another interpretation and suggests a way for the child to address the issue (figure 7.4).

Parents can do more than interpret experiences: they can suggest to children which experiences ought to be included in their self-narrative. Maybe your child concludes, "I'm not much of a reader," because she's comparing herself to her best friend, who happens to be the best reader in the class. Maybe she's thinking of reading only as decoding and needs to be reminded that she's always loved books, and will likely love them again,

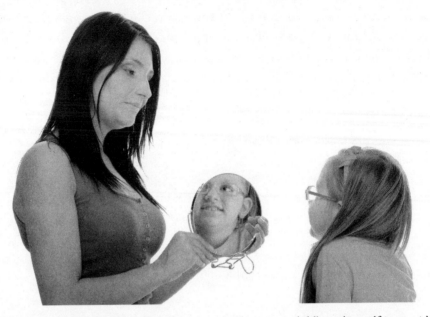

Figure 7.4. Building self-image. If you want to shape your child's reading self-image, it's not enough to simply draw conclusions for her and tell her what she's "really like." She develops her self-image by interpreting her experiences, so you must do the same.
Source: © voyagerix-fotolia.

once the chore of decoding is past. Parents are often children's only source of information about what they were like before age three or so, because none of us remember our earliest years. If your child used to enact bedtime stories with her dolls the next day, she won't have this bit of evidence that she's a reader unless a parent mentions it.

Your Attitude toward Your Child's Reading

It's obvious that your beliefs about your child's reading ability matter—you want to convey confidence that she can be a strong reader, even if she isn't at the moment. Less obvious is the impact of your beliefs about what reading is for. That's worth considering for a moment.

It's natural to think of your child's reading as a skill, because reading does have many properties of skills. It allows you to get certain types

Figure 7.5. Utilitarian view of reading. Perhaps the ultimate advocate of the utilitarian view of reading was Scottish philosopher James Mill, who raised his son, John Stuart Mill (shown here), with the specific aim of genius. John learned Greek at age three and Latin at age eight. The efforts were in some ways successful, as John is known as one of the great philosophers of the nineteenth century, but he later wrote that the intense study imposed by his father had a terrible effect on his mental health.
Source: Wikimedia Commons.

of work done. It improves as you practice. That's true enough, but that view of reading misses another important feature: learning how to read enables entertainment, it enables *fun*. Most of the skills that I teach my children lack that property. I've taught my kids the proper way to clean a bathroom, and I'm pretty sure I did nothing to discourage the idea that cleaning a bathroom is work, a necessary evil. It's worth doing the right way and that brings some satisfaction, but let's not kid ourselves: it's work (figure 7.5).

This attitude is not the one we want to communicate about reading. Reading is not something that you learn to do to be more grown up, or to succeed in school, or to get a job someday. Reading is entertainment. In the rare times that reading feels like work (as when kids are learning to decode), it's work that will enable pleasure later. Research indicates that this attitude on the part of parents is not just associated with higher motivation to read in their children, it is associated with better reading achievement than when parents think of reading as an important school skill.

Obviously this attitude can be communicated explicitly by how you talk about reading. When your child is frustrated because she's having a hard time, you might say, "Well, I know it's hard, but it's hard for everyone. It's just something you have to learn, but it'll get easier," or, "You have to get this down because everything you do in school from now on will depend on it." In contrast, you might say, "Think of how cool it's going to be to read *Cloudy with a Chance of Meatballs* yourself!" or "Think how awesome it's going to be next time we visit Grandma; this time *you* can read *Mr. Popper's Penguins* to *her!*"

Less obvious messages about the nature of reading are conveyed through things you do to get your child to read. For example, suppose you say, "You are not allowed to play with my iPad until you've read at least one chapter in your book." By making something the child wants contingent on reading, you've made it clear that reading is work. The same goes for setting a minimum amount of time that your child must read. You wouldn't say, "I want to see you out on that swing set for at least twenty minutes today, mister. And swing like you mean it." Similarly, no one expects a reward for doing something pleasurable. ("You did such a nice job eating that Snickers, I'm going to give you a dollar.") We expect rewards for doing things that no one would do unless the reward were offered. (School-based reward systems for reading tend to start when kids are a little older, so I discuss them in chapter 10.)

Practice via Practical Literacy

I'm sure you weren't eager to coerce or reward your child, but what if your child doesn't want to read? In chapter 4, I suggested that you change your home environment so that reading is the most attractive activity available, and you can continue that practice. But once your child gains some skill in decoding, you've got another set of options because reading and writing can be practical. The goal is to find situations where he wants to read or write at that moment because it helps him reach a goal. Here are some examples of the kind of thing I mean:

1. Leave your child notes—in his lunchbox, on his bed, in the playhouse, wherever.
2. If your child asks you to convey a message, ask that she write a note instead (figure 7.6).
3. Ask your child to help you with a task that entails reading, and where it's not clear, you could do it yourself (because then you're obviously just quizzing her). For example, in the car: "What's the speed limit around here?" or, "I'm looking for Patrick Street. Help me find it, will you?"
4. Ask your child to bring in the mail and help you out by sorting it by recipient.
5. Show him the cooking directions on a box of pasta (or whatever) and ask him to help you by reading them as you perform each step.
6. Conspire with your child to write a secret note to a sibling or parent.
7. Make writing thank-you notes a habit for your child—not just when she gets a present but when a friend takes her on a special

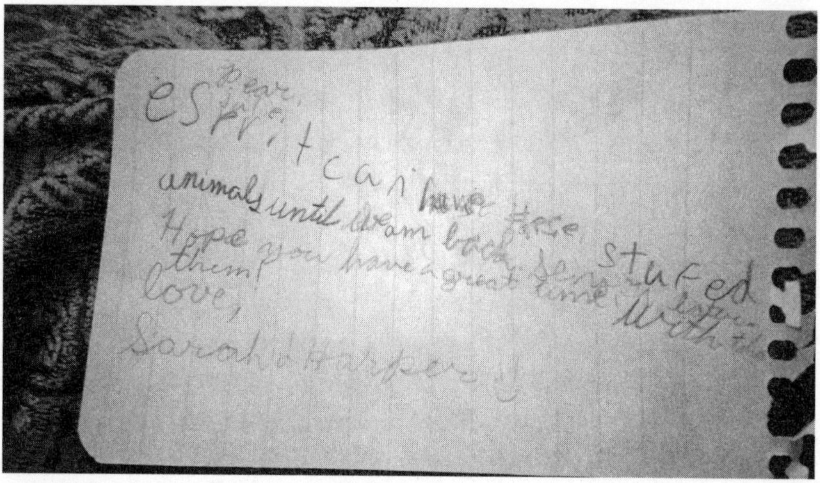

Figure 7.6. The practical value of writing. My daughter, then eight years old, asked me to give a message to her sister's caregiver, who was to arrive later. I said, "I'm sorry, I think I'll be too busy. Can you write her a note?" The text reads: *Dear Julie, Esprit can have these stuffed animals until we am back. Se you later. Hope you have a great time with them! Love, Sarah and Harper.*
Source: © Daniel Willingham.

outing or other activity. Initially you write it and she just signs her name, but as she gains skill, she can write more.

8. When your child gets a new book, make a habit of his writing his name on the inside of the front cover.

9. Encourage writing by buying attractive journals, writing implements, and a case to keep them in. Maybe try markers with a chiseled tip, and show your child how to experiment with varying the width of lines, as in calligraphic writing.

10. Sidewalk chalk (or marking in snow) is a novel way to write. Leave a note for a sibling or parent.

11. Encourage children to write their own cards for birthdays and Christmas.

12. Suggest that your child make a treasure hunt with written clues for a sibling or parent's birthday.

13. Keep a notepad on the refrigerator for a grocery list. When your child asks you to buy some food item, tell him to write it on the list.

14. Instead of the usual coloring books, buy one that includes both art and writing activities. Check for books that are meant to provide summer practice for a particular grade level. But look it over carefully first—they vary in quality quite a bit. Some offer the sort of incidental reading that I'm talking about here, and some are just page after page of drill.

15. On a busy weekend morning, suggest to your child that she make a to-do list for the all the things she has planned for that day—especially if you're making your own list at the same time.

16. In general, try any reading or writing opportunity that has a purpose. For about six months, my youngest thought this was a hilarious way to clean her room: my wife or I would write a brief instruction on a slip of paper (e.g., "Put away toys"), and she'd read it, run off and do it, then return for another note. You never know what will click for your child. But abandon it if you meet resistance. This is for fun, not dull work.

. . . .

The change wrought by learning to decode makes the early elementary years feels grand and impossible to cap. But still bigger changes are to come.

Keeping It Simple Summary

At School

- Good emotional connection between teacher and students
- Teacher modeling enthusiasm for reading
- Finding ways for students to see themselves as successful readers
- Reading accorded a prominent place in the classroom

At Home

- Be an upbeat supporter of your child's growing ability to read.
- Find times that reading or writing serves a useful purpose for your child.
- Maintain an attitude toward reading as a gateway to pleasure, not a skill.

NOTES

"Young children (say, age four or five) tend to see themselves as good at everything": Harter (1999).

"They come to this understanding through comparison.": Ruble and Frey (1991).

"The particular way kids are taught to decode—phonics or whole-word instruction—doesn't affect attitudes.": McKenna, Kear, and Ellsworth (1995).

"happens faster for kids who have a hard time learning to read": Walberg and Tsai (1985).

"putting them in the 'slow' reading group": Wallbrown, Brown, and Engin (1978).

"including good children's literature in a reading program would be associated with more positive attitudes, as would reading aloud to students": Bottomley, Truscott, Marinak, Henk, and Melnick (1999); Morrow (1983, 1992).

"Studies going back to the 1960s have shown that student engagement is driven primarily by the teacher's actions, not the program.": Chall (1967).

"one thousand decisions every school day": Jackson (1968).

"Reading is given a place of prominence": Guthrie and Cox (2001).

"it's helpful when teachers model enthusiasm for reading": Janiuk and Shanahan (1988).

"What you *don't* want to see is endless praise, especially praise that focuses on performance.": Mueller and Dweck (1998).

"that she sees her parents and siblings reading, that there are books in the home, and so forth": Baker, Scher, and Mackler (1997); Braten, Lie, Andreassen, and Olaussen (1999).

"starting when your child is in early elementary school is still a good idea": Villiger, Niggli, Wandeler, and Kutzelmann (2012).

"Kids change their minds about who they are": Grotevant (1987).

"this attitude on the part of parents is not just associated with higher motivation to read in their children": Baker and Scher (2002).

"it is associated with better reading achievement than when parents think of reading as an important school skill": Baker (2003).

PART III

THIRD GRADE AND BEYOND

8

READING WITH FLUENCY

Your child is now a third grader or older. Assuming all has gone more or less to plan, doesn't he know how to decode by this age? He does, but there are actually *two* processes of decoding, not one. The first process, more easily observed, develops in kindergarten. The second process, clandestine, develops slowly and is still being fine-tuned as late as high school. It's this second process that supports fluency, and it's just as important as the first process, for it enables your child to read quickly and effortlessly. In this chapter, we look at ways to ensure it develops in full.

THE SECOND TYPE OF DECODING: READING VIA SPELLING

So far I have described decoding as the process by which the reader turns printed letters into sound. I said beginning readers *don't* recognize words by their appearance—that is, by their spelling. But we can think of cases where it would seem that spelling must count for something. If reading depended only on sound, how could you differentiate homophones like "knight" and "night"? You could argue that you use sound to read the word, but then you use the meaning of the sentence to figure out whether "knight" or "night" is meant. Thus, when you read the line from Sandburg's poem "Night from a railroad car window is a great, dark, soft thing," you know the poet is talking about the evening because a mounted soldier in armor is unlikely to be seen from a railroad car. But if I use surrounding context to disambiguate meaning, then it shouldn't be noticeable if I encounter the phrase, "My favorite Beatles album is *A Hard Day's Knight*" or a reference to a strongman performing "feets of strength." Spelling, it seems, does matter to reading.

It turns out that experienced readers have two ways of accessing word meaning from print. The first is the way I've already described: you use a set of rules to translate the printed letters to sound, and then more or less say the word to yourself. The sound of the word is connected to its meaning. The second method uses the spelling: you directly match letters on the page to your knowledge of how words are spelled. That spelling knowledge is also connected to the meaning (figure 8.1).

Fluency and Attention

The spelling knowledge you use to read is a bit like your ability to recognize objects in that you don't need to consciously consider what things look like to recognize them. You don't say to yourself, "Hmm, let's see . . . there's a paw, and that looks sort of like a muzzle, and that thing is probably a tail . . . this is shaping up to be a dog." You just see a dog. And like your ability to recognize objects, your ability to visually recognize words includes being able to recognize pieces; even though you seldom encounter a dog's paw in isolation, you would know that it's a paw. Likewise, spelling

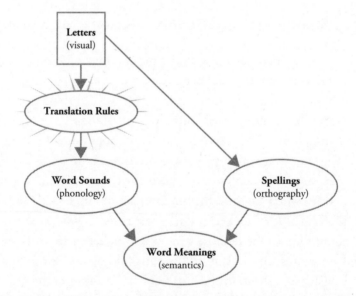

Figure 8.1. Two reading pathways. There are two ways to get from print on the page to meaning in your mind. A complete diagram would include other connections—expecting a particular meaning influences what you hear, for example—but we'll keep things simple.
Source: © Daniel Willingham.

representations in the mind can identify clumps of letters that you frequently see, even though they are typically part of a word. That's why "fage" looks more like a word than "fajy." The letter "j" is seldom followed by the letter "y," but "ge" is a frequently encountered clump of letters.

Reading by spelling does allow you to differentiate homophones like "knight" and "night," but there's a much more important advantage: it's faster and easier to use than the translation rules. Translation rules demand a lot of attention (symbolized by the radiating lines in figure 8.1). Just as the beginner driving a car must consciously think about how far to turn the steering wheel to change lanes, how closely he's following the car ahead, and so on, the attention of the beginning reader is absorbed by sounding words out: "Let's see, 'o' usually sounds like AW, but when there are two of them, 'oo,' they make a different sound . . . what was it again?" That makes it hard to focus on understanding the meaning of what she's reading.

With experience, all of that thinking the driver had to do seems to disappear. Driving becomes automatic, and you can stay in your lane and keep the car at the correct speed without really thinking about it. That leaves your attention free to do something else: daydream or talk with a passenger, for example. In the same way, practice in reading reduces the attentional demand imposed by translation rules—reduces, but never completely eliminates. You can feel the small attentional cost yourself when you encounter an unfamiliar word and sound it out; for a short one like "fey," the cost may be barely noticeable, but make the word long so that it really taxes the translation process, and you notice that your reading slows down. Try "triskaidekaphobia."

In contrast, using word spellings to read requires very little attention, if any. You just see it in the same way you just see and recognize a dog. As your child gains reading experience, there is a larger and larger set of words that he can read using the spelling, and so his reading becomes faster, smoother, and more accurate. That's called *fluency*.

Fluency and Prosody

It's easy to see that fluency would aid comprehension. With sound translation demanding less attention, more attention can be paid to meaning. There's a second, somewhat more subtle way that fluency helps

Let's eat, Grandma!

Let's eat Grandma!

Punctuation. It saves lives.

Figure 8.2. Prosody and meaning. This grammar joke has made the rounds on
Facebook. In school we learn where to place commas based on grammar, but most of us
don't use them that way when we read. Instead, the comma carries auditory signifi-
cance. It signals an accent just before the comma and a pause after—hence, LET'S *EAT*. . .
GRANDMA. In the second case we hear LET'S EAT *GRAND*MA.
Source: © Daniel Willingham.

comprehension. Fluency actually ends up helping comprehension through
sound. Here's how.

I mentioned prosody in chapter 2 when discussing "motherese." You'll
recall that it's the sort of melody of speech. We don't speak in a monotone;
words vary in pitch, pacing, and emphasis. This melody carries meaning. If I
say, "What a great party," with enthusiasm or with sarcasm, the words are the
same. Only the prosody differs. Prosody helps you differentiate sarcasm from
enthusiasm; it also helps with the essential but less glamorous donkey work
of comprehension, namely, assigning grammatical roles to words (figure 8.2).

Even when you read silently, you add prosodic information to help
you comprehend. Poet Billy Collins put it more eloquently: "I think when
you're reading in silence you actually hear the poem in your head because
the skull is like a little auditorium." If you're reading fluently, access to individual words requires almost no attention, and that means you have more
attention to devote to working out the prosody. Indeed, some research
indicates that it is the development of prosody, and not the reading rate
itself, that leads to the boost in reading comprehension associated with fluency (figure 8.3).

Figure 8.3. The silent reader. St. Ambrose, depicted in this statue on the Giureconsulti Palace in Milan, was a fourth-century archbishop of that city. St. Augustine famously noted that Ambrose read silently: "When he read, his eyes scanned the page and his heart sought out the meaning, but his voice was silent and his tongue was still." Some scholars have taken this passage as evidence that people at that time typically read aloud. That hypothesis matches the fact that punctuation was then used only sporadically; vocalizing would help the reader hear the prosody.
Source: Photo by Giovanni Dall-Orto, Wikimedia Commons. http://commons.wikimedia.org/wiki/Saint
_Ambrose#mediaviewer/File:IMG_3106_-_Milano_-_Sant%27Ambrogio_sul_Palazzo_dei_Giureconsulti
_-_Foto_di_Giovanni_Dall%27Orto_3-gen-2007.jpg

Fluency allows for better comprehension of what you read. And fluency depends on being able to read via spelling. So how do you learn to do that?

Learning to Read via Spelling

I start by clarifying what might have sounded like a contradiction. In chapter 5, I wrote, "It doesn't work very well to teach reading by encouraging children to memorize what words look like. You have to teach the sound-translation rules." Now I'm concluding that "reading by spelling is essential to good reading." But these ideas don't really contradict one another. Memorizing what words look like is impractical for learning to read, but once children know how to read, they teach themselves how to read via spelling.

Suppose I were trying to train a child to recognize words by their spellings. I might show her the word "dog" and tell her, "That word is dog." Then I show her the word "log," and tell her, "That word is log." The child who can decode doesn't need me to tell her the identity of each printed word. She tells herself. When she decodes a word using the sound mechanism, she's identifying which word she's seeing and she's seeing the letter pattern at the same time. With enough repetitions, the spelling of the word and its identity come to be associated.

This is called the self-teaching hypothesis. Most kids are taught how to sound words out, but they teach themselves (without knowing they are doing so) what words look like, based on practice distributed over several years. It's hard to give a firm estimate of exactly how long it takes to become a fluent reader. For one thing, fluency is graded. It's not that you're fluent or you're not; it's that your reading slowly becomes more and more fluent, so defining a time you've reached the goal is a little arbitrary. That said, the first stage of fluency is noticeable; there is some point at which a child seems to have turned a corner—she is no longer painstakingly sounding out each word but is instead reading. That might come after, say, six to nine months of decoding practice. And that's another thing that makes it hard to come up with an estimate of when it will happen. It's not the passage of time that's crucial; it's what's happening during that time. Fluency will come faster or slower depending on how much reading the child does. The more frequently she encounters a word, the richer her knowledge of what it looks like.

What's Happening at School

The main mechanism to develop fluency is reading. As in younger grades, reading aloud with feedback is preferable to silent reading, but that may become less practicable in many classrooms as kids get older because their reading competence diverges more. Fortunately, reading aloud is somewhat less important (compared to when students were learning to decode) because competent decoders can provide mostly accurate feedback to themselves.

It would be nice to get kids to fluency faster, especially given that national tests indicate only about half of kids have reached desired levels of fluency by fourth grade. Is there a way to hurry the process along?

Three techniques can help. First, explicit spelling instruction seems to improve fluency. Although the spelling knowledge you use to read is not identical to the knowledge you use when you're thinking about how to spell a word, there is some overlap. So that's a reason to include spelling instruction in schools, even though we all use word processors with spell-checkers (figure 8.4).

A second technique that can help students develop fluency is for the teacher to model reading with prosody. If reading with the right melody is the mechanism by which fluency helps comprehension, then students should know what they are aiming toward. Note too that this is still another benefit of parents' reading aloud to their children, even as they get older. It might also help for kids to occasionally hear *negative* examples— the teacher reading as fast as possible, for example, or in a robotic voice.

Figure 8.4. Spelling matters. Spelling instruction seems to promote fluency, but there are other reasons spelling is important. For example, tattoo machines don't come with spell-check.

Source: © doris oberfrank-list—Fotolia. Modified from the image.

A third technique to develop fluency is repeated reading. The child reads the same text enough times so that he can do so fluently. As when an adult models prosody, the idea is to give him a better idea of what fluent, prosodic reading sounds like, so he knows what he's trying to do.

The research evidence for these techniques is not terribly strong, however; sometimes they seem to work, and sometimes they don't. It may be that when the interventions were tested, they have not been of sufficient duration, or it may be that some kids had other reading issues that were preventing them from getting the full benefit of fluency. But researchers have had less success with in-school training regimens for fluency than when they've targeted other reading processes.

What to Do at Home

Even if the main prescription for fluency—"tons of reading"—seems obvious, how to get older kids to engage in tons of reading is not. Let's look at what parents can do to get reluctant older kids to read.

Is There a Problem?

Before you consider your role in helping your child develop reading fluency, you need some sense of how it's going. His school likely monitored reading closely in the early grades, but once he learned to decode fairly well, that monitoring probably tapered off. You too may have thought that the process of learning to read was pretty much done and that your child was all set. And now, when he's older, if he seems to do his assigned reading and his teacher is satisfied, you wouldn't have had much reason to question whether he's a fluent reader.

You can get a sense of your child's reading fluency by asking him to read aloud. Fluent reading will be expressive, whereas dysfluent reading will sound robotic, expressionless. The fluent reader will pause at places that sound natural, conversational. Dysfluent reading has pauses, but the reading sounds halting—you can hear that the reader is stuck on a word and is figuring it out. A fluent reader seldom loses his place while reading, and, when reading silently, he doesn't move his mouth much. A dysfluent reader does both.

If his reading is dysfluent, that doesn't necessarily mean he's dyslexic. It probably means he needs more practice than other kids to develop fluency and hasn't had it yet. And given that reading is effortful, he gets less pleasure from reading and therefore avoids it. That means practice is unlikely without a little push.

What Does a Dysfluent Reader Need?

Some parents I have known simply charged ahead and required that their child practice reading. If that's you, the same approach I described in chapter 5 applies: brief daily sessions (five or ten minutes) with age-appropriate support and enthusiasm from you, along with a good dose of persistence to ensure that it happens. Some parents use a clever method to ensure practice; their child is allowed to watch thirty minutes of television each day but beyond that it can only be watched with the volume muted and closed captioning on.

If you take this direct route, it's worth thinking about how you will talk to your child about the need for practice. Not many kids will respond well to a logical argument about the value of reading. Anything you might tell them, they already know. In fact, they know quite well that being a reader is associated with intelligence, and many will see their halting reading as evidence that they are just not that smart. (In fact, the opposite is probably true. Anyone who earns passing grades without being a strong reader probably has a good memory and reasons well.)

The point of reading practice is not the correction of a defect in your child. Rather, you are hoping to enrich her life. I think about reading much the way I think about food. Why don't I let my child eat mostly mac-and-cheese and carrot sticks? Because even though she believes she'd be perfectly happy on that limited diet, I think that eating affords some of the most transcendent pleasures available. Of course, I want that for my child. In the same way, I want her to have access, through reading, to the greatest minds of history. A child who has long felt indifferent to reading won't see it that way, but if you explain your motivation, she will at least understand that you are not criticizing her for some lack. Your goal is not for her to be a good reader; it's that she enjoy reading.

The Indirect Route

I know some parents wouldn't feel comfortable trying to get their teen to practice reading; how well that's going to work obviously depends on your relationship and your history with your child. You can also try an indirect method with reading activities that demand less of her and are harder to say no to. These ideas won't work for all families, but maybe one or two would work for yours.

You could try a family reading time once a week, in which each person reads silently together. Pitch it as a weekly time away from screens and with one another. If your child tries to show you that she doesn't have to play along (perhaps by selecting baby books or catalogues), ignore it. She may actually be selecting books from early childhood both because she remembers them fondly and because they are easy to read. For this reason, don't be quick to give away books your child has outgrown.

A related idea is to have the whole family listen together to an audiobook of mutual interest—and from there perhaps to one family member reading aloud to the others. Obviously the stated goal is not to practice reading. The motivation is that reading is pleasurable, spending time together as a family is pleasurable, and this is a way to do both. Time is always a problem, but even if you start with just fifteen minutes each week, that's more than nothing, and the hope is that an interesting book will prompt some sessions to go longer. Needless to say, it's a good idea to start with the most appealing book you can think of (figure 8.5). More on that in chapter 10.

You can also begin visits to the library even if you've never gotten into this habit before. If your child doesn't want to go, tell him *you* need to go, and say that the most convenient time for you is during a trip to take him somewhere he needs to go.

It's true that these reading scenarios are pretty contrived. You should also be on the lookout for times that it's logical for your child to read. If there is a younger sibling in the house, that child should be read to: the older child might take that on. (She might also read to the children of friends who visit.) Such reading is a nice chance for your child to revisit favorites from childhood and perhaps awaken memories of reading that are more pleasant than the recent ones.

Figure 8.5. Charles Dickens reading aloud to his daughters. If you institute family read-alouds, you might want to make things a bit less formal.

Source: http://commons.wikimedia.org/wiki/File:Charles_Dickens_with_his_two_daughters_by_Mason_& _Co_%28Robert_Hindry_Mason%29.jpg.

I find good opportunities for my children to read when one of them wants something. When our daughter wanted an aquarium, my wife and I said, "Okay, if you're going to take care of it, you have to learn about them." So she got a book and read up on aquaria. The same argument can be made for nearly anything: a tree house, a green belt in karate, or a driver's license.

A rather sneaky motivator is this implicit bargain: "if my child is reading, I will do my utmost not to interrupt him." That sounds natural, but if the principle extends to moments where you would typically ask the child's help around the house, then it could become a useful motivator. Of course, it is essential that you not make this bargain explicit.

It will be turned down, or you will end up quibbling about what sort of reading material "counts" or whether the chores were invented so as to persuade the child to read. If you leave it unstated, it may be a while before your child puts together what's going on, and that leaves you with much better options for how to implement it.

For some students, a forceful external motivation to improve their reading pops up unexpectedly. I once met a high schooler who was an avid baseball player. Sophomore year he made varsity but not first string, and he concluded he probably could not make a living as a player. He started to think about coaching or perhaps working in the front office of a minor league team. He did some research and learned he was much more likely to get a job with a degree in sports management. More or less overnight he became keenly interested in academic work so he could go to college. He realized that some of the struggle was getting through his textbooks, so he began to work on his reading.

Digital Difference

If your child is an uncertain reader, you might wonder whether extensive experience with digital media is somehow impoverishing her reading. There's little indication that reading on a screen is substantially different from reading on paper.

Research does show that the way a book is put on the screen can affect comprehension, but the effects are relatively modest. For example, comprehension is better if you navigate a book by flipping virtual pages, compared to scrolling. And clickable links (hyperlinks) incur a cost to comprehension even if you don't click them. Because you can see that they are clickable, you still need to make a decision about whether to click. That draws on your attention and so carries a cost to comprehension. But most of these effects are small, so if you're wondering whether your child would enjoy reading more on an e-reader (or whether reading on such a device is frustrating him), I'd say "probably not."

There is one qualification to that conclusion. If your child's school is considering moving to electronic textbooks, be at least a little wary. Publishers are working to improve electronic textbooks, but with the current offerings, the research is pretty consistently negative. Comprehension is about the same as when reading on paper, but reading is less efficient. It takes longer to read electronic textbooks, and it feels more effortful. Quite consistently, a majority of students who have used electronic textbooks say they would rather use paper. The problem is probably not due to greater difficulty decoding an electronic book; the problem is that reading for pleasure is different from reading for school. The information is structured differently, it's more complex, and you're reading it to learn and remember it, not just to enjoy it.

This greater complexity and the demand that students do more with textbooks characterize the reading challenges that begin in upper elementary school. In the next chapter, we turn out attention to these complications.

Keeping It Simple Summary

At School

- Practice reading to develop fluency.
- Strategies like repeated reading or the teacher modeling prosodic reading may help, but the research support is tenuous.

At Home

- Encourage reading practice for the child who is a halting reader (though not dyslexic).
- If direct practice seems unworkable, look for ways that reading can logically creep into your child's day.

Notes

"it also helps with the essential but less glamorous donkey work of comprehension": Carlson (2009).

"'the skull is like a little auditorium'": Rehm (2013).

"it is the development of prosody, and not reading rate itself, that leads to the boost in reading comprehension associated with fluency": Veenendaal, Groen, and Verhoeven (2014).

"the self-teaching hypothesis": Share (1995).

"based on practice distributed over several years": Grainger, Lété, Bertand, Dufau, and Ziegler (2012).

"The more frequently she encounters a word, the richer your knowledge of what it looks like.": Arciuli and Simpson (2012); Kessler (2009).

"The main mechanism to develop fluency is reading.": Collins and Levy (2008); Ehri (2008).

"national tests indicate only about half of kids have reached desired levels of fluency by fourth grade": Daane, Campbell, Grigg, Goodman, and Oranje (2005).

"explicit spelling instruction seems to improve fluency": Shanahan and Lomax (1986).

"A second technique that can help students develop fluency is for the teacher to model reading with prosody.": See, for example, Dowhower (1989).

"A third technique to develop fluency is repeated reading." Samuels (1979).

"The research evidence for these techniques is not terribly strong": Breznitz and Share (1992); Fleisher, Jenkins, and Pany (1979); Tan and Nicholson (1997).

"comprehension is better if you navigate a book by flipping virtual pages, compared to scrolling": Sanchez and Wiley (2009).

"clickable links (hyperlinks) incur a cost to comprehension": DeStefano and LeFevre (2007).

"Comprehension is about the same as when reading on paper, but reading is less efficient.": Connell, Bayliss, and Farmer (2012); Daniel and Woody (2013); Rockinson-Szapkiw, Courduff, Carter, and Bennett (2013); Schugar, Schugar, and Penny (2011).

"It takes longer to read electronic textbooks, and it feels more effortful.": Ackerman and Goldsmith (2011); Ackerman and Lauterman (2012); Connell et al. (2012); Daniel and Woody (2013).

"reading for pleasure is different from reading for school": For more on how reading for pleasure is different from reading for schools as it applies to e-textbooks, see Daniel and Willingham (2012).

9

Working with More Complex Texts

The truism has it that children "first learn to read, and then read to learn." Your third grader can decode, so presumably it's time to "read to learn." That catchphrase is a bit deceptive however, as it simplifies what is actually a quite serious increase in the expectations for comprehension.

What's Happening at School

"Read to learn" makes comprehension sound so straightforward, but by this point, you know that comprehension rests on three factors:

1. The reader must know the definitions of most of the words used in the text.
2. The reader must be able to assign syntactic roles to sentences, which could be difficult if they are long or if the syntax is convoluted.
3. Writers inevitably omit some information that's needed to relate sentences to one another. The reader must have relevant background knowledge to fill these gaps.

Note that all three are characteristics of either the text *or* of the reader. That is, a writer can make a text more comprehensible by using simple vocabulary and straightforward syntax, and by assuming little background knowledge on the part of the reader. If the writer doesn't do these things, the reader is not completely defenseless. The reader can look up words she doesn't know, she can expend more mental effort to untangle difficult syntax, and (although this one is tougher) she can try to find the knowledge that's necessary to make appropriate inferences. But before the reader will do that extra work, she must first recognize, "Hey, I don't understand this."

Noticing When Comprehension Fails

How hard can it be to perceive that you don't understand what you're reading? Students are not as good at this work as you might think. They notice if a word is not in their vocabulary. They notice if they don't understand the syntax of a sentence. But they don't always connect the meaning of sentences, and they don't notice that they fail to do so. That's especially true of poor readers, who are satisfied with a fairly minimal understanding of a text; when something goes wrong with their comprehension, they often don't try to solve the problem. It's not that they are unable to make appropriate inferences. Have them watch an engrossing movie, for example, and they will draw inferences to understand each scene and will think about how scenes fit together so they can follow the plot. But when they read, they figure that if they know most of the words and understand individual sentences, then they are doing their job (figure 9.1).

Figure 9.1. Movies require complex inferences. A ten-year-old who can follow a complex movie plot should be able to read a comparably complex text, provided he can decode well.
Source: © Rach via Flickr. https://www.flickr.com/photos/vagueonthehow/3774991334/in
/photolist-54YrBY-4ZfWpn-51Cnrk-4ZtVhj-512Aiu-4Xxhk2–4XhLcn-4XR7vG-51gwnW-5j2jvc
-4XQWws-5kWw1p-56UHcC-6yGW7e-4SiUyg-56QwCk-56UE4A-56QC1i-bsLKHh-9RptqD-4YDHmd
-GENpu-5pec4v-68sUVG-9MwpGD-7rVXe8–6B9Cmm-2mUFw8–6KzPpu-6KVGw-5pZtEH-jRZ6Y6
-ifXqaC-ipa6hz-4VFvcT-2gHAQR-8UFRXk-9xFA2W-6QLQeF-8MaJJT-8f9EeK-93t1mC-7fBLn-6KVGx
-2jkwer-8WNwyv-2eoXoy-oujHCq-hNfG1L-otTJio.

I know it seems strange and the research showing this phenom-enon would almost be funny if not for the pathos. For example, in one experiment, sixth graders were asked to read essays at the request of an experimenter who told them she needed help to make the essays clearer for children. The essays contained ideas that contradicted one another. Sometimes the contradictions were subtle, as in this example:

> "There is absolutely no light at the bottom of the ocean. Some fish that live at the bottom of the ocean know their food by color. They will only eat red fungus."

In other essays, the contradiction was made very explicit:

> "Fish must have light in order to see. There is absolutely no light at the bottom of the ocean. It is pitch black down there. When it is that dark the fish cannot see anything. They cannot even see colors. Some fish that live at the bottom of the ocean can see the color of their food; that is how they know what to eat."

Remarkably, when the error was subtle, sixth graders noticed it no more than 10 percent of the time. Even when it was made terribly obvious, no more than half noticed it.

Reading Comprehension Strategies

What would happen if you told students, "Hey, you should really try to tie the meaning of sentences together?" And while we're at it, we can tell them that their background knowledge will be helpful in making those connec-tions and that they must evaluate whether the connections they are drawing seem to make sense. These are the core ideas behind *reading comprehen-sion strategies*, a mainstay of reading education in upper elementary school and beyond. You don't just tell students to "tie the meaning of sentences together," because that's a bit vague. Instead you give them more concrete tasks—tasks that can't be completed unless you connect the sentences.

Here's a list of commonly taught reading comprehension strategies. (You won't be quizzed on them, so feel free to skim.)

1. **Comprehension monitoring.** Readers are taught to become aware of when they do not understand, for example, by describing what exactly is causing them difficulty.
2. **Listening actively.** Students learn to think critically as they listen and to appreciate that listening involves understanding a message from the speaker.
3. **Prior knowledge.** Students are encouraged to apply what they know from their own lives to the text or to consider the theme of the text before reading it.
4. **Vocabulary-comprehension relationship.** Students are encouraged to use background knowledge (as well as textual clues) to make educated guesses about the meaning of unfamiliar words.
5. **Graphic organizer.** Students learn how to make graphic representations of texts, for example, story maps.
6. **Question answering.** After students read a text, the teacher poses questions that emphasize the information students should have obtained from the text.
7. **Question generation.** Students are taught to generate their own questions as they read, with the goal of summarizing major themes of the text.
8. **Summarization.** Students are taught techniques of summarizing (e.g., deleting redundant information) and choosing a topic sentence for the main idea.
9. **Mental imagery.** Students are instructed to create a mental visual image based on the text.
10. **Cooperative learning.** Students enact comprehension strategies—for example, prediction and summarization—in small groups rather than with the teacher.
11. **Story structure.** Students are taught the typical structure of a story, and learn how to create a story map.

Note that these reading comprehension strategies encourage students to do exactly what we said is required for comprehension. Strategies 1 and 2 are designed to get students monitoring their comprehension. Strategies 3 and 4 are meant to get students to relate their prior knowledge to what they read. And strategies 5 through 11 require relating sentences in the text to one another.

Figure 9.2. Do adults use reading strategies? Who sits down at the breakfast table and thinks, "Ah, here's a headline about Ukraine. Let me activate my background knowledge about Eastern Europe in preparation to read this article"? Of course, it's possible that I used to use these strategies, but after years of reading, they've become automatic and I don't notice that I use them.
Source: © Daniel Willingham.

If you're an experienced reader, these strategies may seem like unnecessary complications (figure 9.2). Nevertheless, teaching these strategies to students is supported by research. Here's the way a typical experiment works. You administer a reading test to some students, say, fourth graders. Then you teach them a reading comprehension strategy. Most often, you wouldn't teach them just one: you'd teach a combination of perhaps three. Over the course of a few weeks, you'd have a number of sessions (from as few as ten to as many as fifty or more) in which you'd model how to use the strategies and the students would practice. The sessions might be daily or a few times per week. At the end of the experiment you would administer a reading test again and see whether comprehension has improved. (You'd compare the improvement to a control group of students who were not taught the strategy.)

Many studies show that teaching strategies improves reading comprehension, and the gains are by no means trivial. The exact size of the boost is complicated to calculate, but even the low estimates have this relatively brief intervention—as short as a few weeks—moving a child reading at the 50th percentile up to the 64th percentile.*

A Little Is Enough

The documented benefit of reading comprehension strategy instruction is impressive given its modest cost, yet this instruction is easy to overdo. Teaching reading strategies does work, but the benefit comes after just a few sessions, and it doesn't get any bigger with more practice.

Here's how we know that. Suppose you looked at fifty experiments that had taught kids reading comprehension strategies. In some experiments, kids got just a few lessons in how to use them. In other experiments, kids got more practice. You would expect that more practice would lead to bigger gains in reading. But it doesn't. Just a few sessions—five or ten—give the same benefit as fifty. That finding, which several researchers have observed, is hard to square with the idea that reading comprehension strategies directly improve comprehension. We have this idea that comprehension is a skill, like hitting a baseball, and comprehension strategies are like things that the coach tells you: "Keep your eye on the ball," "Your hips provide the power of the swing," and so on. We practice these strategies, and our skill improves.

---

*I say that the size of the effect is hard to calculate for several reasons. For some strategies, there aren't enough studies to be sure, and for others, the size of the effect depends on the measure of reading. Some researchers use a standardized reading test, whereas others create their own test. Reading strategy instruction appears to have a bigger effect when experimenters write the test. That doesn't mean that those who create their own reading tests are consciously stacking the deck in their favor. If a researcher thinks that teaching students to summarize will help their reading comprehension, it's only natural that he will create a reading test that emphasizes summaries. The figures I cite are the lower estimates, which I think is fairer.

ASSEMBLY INSTRUCTIONS

1. Don't just fit parts together; remember you're building something big.

2. Thinking about how you have put things together before will help you put together this object now.

3. Every so often you should look at what you're building, and evaluate how it's going.

Figure 9.3. Furniture assembly strategy instructions.
Source: © Joe Gough—Fotolia.

But remember how comprehension works. It depends on the particular content of sentences, so it's not open to that kind of strategic instruction. Here's an analogy. Suppose that reading is like putting together a piece of furniture you bought at Ikea. Like a text, furniture has parts that must fit together in a particular way, and if you do the job right, all the parts coalesce into something larger—a functional object.

Suppose you lay out all the pieces of your unassembled desk, and find strategy-like instructions (figure 9.3). These instructions don't tell you how to actually build the piece of furniture. You need to know whether piece A is supposed to attach to piece B or C. Rather, these instructions concern what to think about when you're executing instructions (the ones that tell you that part A attaches to part B).

Reading comprehension strategies are similar. They tell you what to do: monitor your comprehension, relate prior knowledge to what you're reading, relate sentences in the text to one another. They don't tell you how to get those things done. They *can't*, because how to do them depends on the particulars. Comprehension requires relating sentence A to sentence B, but I can't give you generic instructions about how to relate them. Their relationship depends on the contents of sentence A and sentence B.

For someone who thinks that assembling furniture is merely a matter of attaching pieces to one another for a while, this big-picture overview is good advice. Likewise, if a child doesn't appreciate that the purpose of reading is communication and that she's meant to understand what she reads, comprehension strategy instruction is a great idea. For example, a student who has difficulty decoding may view decoding as synonymous with reading. Decoding is really taxing, so if I'm decoding, then I'm doing my job. Reading comprehension strategy instruction tells the child, "Decoding is not enough. You are supposed to understand what you're reading. Just as you do when you listen to a story, when you read, you must relate the beginning, middle, and end."

A New Demand: Working with Texts

The National Assessment of Educational Progress, more commonly known as the "Nation's Report Card," defines "basic" fourth-grade reading skill as the ability to "locate relevant information, make simple inferences, and use their understanding of the text to identify details that support a given interpretation or conclusion." In other words, comprehension is no longer defined as understanding the text. Comprehension means being able to use the text to aid reasoning. And of course texts become longer and more complex with each grade. If that weren't enough, upper elementary and middle school is when teachers often start to expect that students will do more reading independently at home, so that class time can be devoted to other things.

Later, in high school, students may learn that researchers in different disciplines treat texts differently. It's not just that researchers know different things and are interested in different facets of a text. Each discipline has norms about what's interesting and important. For example, sourcing is fundamental to a historian's work: Who wrote this text, with what goal in mind, and for what audience? Scientists care little, if at all, about sourcing or the author's perspective. But budding scientists must learn how scientific journal articles are structured: what goes into the methods section, what sort of speculation is permissible in the discussion section, and so forth. As students learn more about a discipline, they learn what merits special attention according to the conventions of the discipline and what is secondary (figure 9.4).

"Comprehension" comes to mean different things as students get older. Initially it means no more than "understand the story." Later, we want students to put texts to other purposes: find facts for research, memorize information for a test, or analyze the author's technique to persuade or evoke emotion. Students who were strong readers in early grades may find themselves challenged as they had not been before by these tasks.

```
                                        Albert Einstein
                                        Old Grove Rd.
                                        Nassau Point
                                        Peconic, Long Island
                                        August 2nd, 1939

F.D. Roosevelt,
President of the United States,
White House
Washington, D.C.

     Sir:

         Some recent work by E.Fermi and L. Szilard, which has been com-
     municated to me in manuscript, leads me to expect that the element uran-
     ium may be turned into a new and important source of energy in the im-
     mediate future. Certain aspects of the situation which has arisen seem
     to call for watchfulness and, if necessary, quick action on the part
     of the Administration. I believe therefore that it is my duty to bring
     to your attention the following facts and recommendations:

         In the course of the last four months it has been made probable -
     through the work of Joliot in France as well as Fermi and Szilard in
     America - that it may become possible to set up a nuclear chain reaction
     in a large mass of uranium,by which vast amounts of power and large quant-
     ities of new radium-like elements would be generated. Now it appears
     almost certain that this could be achieved in the immediate future.

         This new phenomenon would also lead to the construction of bombs,
     and it is conceivable - though much less certain - that extremely power-
     ful bombs of a new type may thus be constructed. A single bomb of this
     type, carried by boat and exploded in a port, might very well destroy
     the whole port together with some of the surrounding territory. However,
     such bombs might very well prove to be too heavy for transportation by
     air.

                              a64a01
```

Figure 9.4. Historic letter. This is the first page of a letter from Albert Einstein to President Roosevelt about the possibility of developing atomic bombs. This letter would be read in different ways by a historian, a scientist, and a theologian.
Source: WikiMedia Commons, http://commons.wikimedia.org/wiki/File:Einstein_Szilard_p1.jpg.

Most of this work happens at school, not at home, but it's useful for parents to have it on their radar. You want to be aware that your child is taking on these new tasks and to ensure that he is getting the proper instruction and support at school. The teacher may assume that students have learned something—how to use reference materials, for example—in an earlier grade, when in fact your child never received that instruction. (That's obviously a greater risk if you switched schools.) It's best to be in touch with your child's teacher so that you know what she's doing in class and can ask how you can support this work at home.

Digital Literacy

Some education commentators have suggested that we need to think of "reading comprehension" differently, because it (along with writing and other aspects of literacy) has been so profoundly changed by the broad availability of digital technologies. The ability to create, navigate, and evaluate information on various digital platforms is generically called "digital literacy." What should we make of this? Is the idea of "reading comprehension" outdated?

Different aspects of digital literacy need to be evaluated separately. Consider first the idea of a general tech savviness. I think there's little doubt that exposure to and practice with digital technologies teach kids certain conventions common across these technologies: menuing systems, hierarchical file structures, and the like. This knowledge is important exactly because these conventions are respected across applications and across devices. But they are pretty easy to learn. Software is engineered to be simple to use, and kids learn this stuff rapidly. Some adults like to joke about how helpless they are in the face of these newfangled gadgets compared to kids who seem such naturals. But kids in fact vary widely in their tech knowledge, and age-related differences, when they exist, are not due to limited learning abilities on the part of oldsters; they are due to youngsters' greater motivation and opportunities to learn from their peers.

The second aspect of digital literacy is the ability to evaluate information. The web is often praised for its effect in democratizing publishing. Twenty years ago, the owners of publishing companies were gatekeepers of information. My comprehensive knowledge of, say, rare animal species in the Pacific Northwest would remain unknown if I could not persuade the gatekeepers to publish it. Now I can publish whatever I like over the web or as an e-book and let consumers decide whether it's valuable. That's great, but the gatekeepers did serve a function: most had an interest in ensuring some quality control. Certainly they fulfilled this role imperfectly—falsehoods were and are published by mainstream sources—but as standing institutions, publishers are more accountable than individuals publishing websites on a lark, and their records for accuracy are easier to track. On the web, readers must take greater responsibility for evaluating the reliability of what they encounter.

Figure 9.5. Tree octopus. A screenshot from the website describing the fictitious tree octopus.

Source: http://zapatopi.net/treeoctopus/.

In the mid-2000s the need for greater student education on this matter gained publicity through a website describing the endangered Northwest Tree Octopus, a fictitious species said to live in trees (figure 9.5). The website deftly mimics the prose used in science textbooks ("Because of the moistness of the rainforests and specialized skin adaptations, they are able to keep from becoming desiccated for prolonged periods of time."). Aside from the absurdity of a cephalopod living out of water, there are hints scattered throughout that it's a hoax—for example, the octopus's main predator is said to be the sasquatch, and the website is endorsed by the organization "Greenpeas."

Yet when researchers at the University of Connecticut asked twenty-five seventh graders to evaluate the site—students named by their schools as their most proficient online readers—every single one fell for the hoax. When they were told that it was false, most struggled to find evidence that could have told them that, and some even insisted that website was legitimate. Other research has shown that students rarely critically evaluate information they find on the web. They probably would be no more critical of a paper pamphlet on the tree octopus; the point is that there is more misinformation on the web than is generated by traditional publishers, and so kids need to be more discerning when reading there.

In the last few years, there have been greater efforts to teach students how to be critical readers of information on the web. Students have been taught techniques like evaluating the author's credentials, tracing the domain to evaluate whether the website is commercial or originates in the education community, checking how recently the web page was updated, and looking for other websites that have linked back to the target site. Teaching students these evaluation skills is still in its infancy, but thus far it has been tough going. Some studies indicate that it helps students understand the importance of evaluating websites, but their evaluations of websites don't actually improve.

WHAT TO DO AT HOME

As before, most of what I've encouraged you to do by way of making your home knowledge rich and your child knowledge hungry still applies. This age does bring two new concerns. First, most kids begin to spend significant amounts of time with digital devices, so we'll evaluate what that might mean for acquiring background knowledge. Second, we need to consider strategies you might employ if you think that a lack of background knowledge is impairing your child's reading comprehension.

Knowledge in the Digital Age

As kids move into middle school, they don't just spend more time with digital devices; they also change what they do with them. They still watch a lot of video content, but they add video gaming, texting, and surfing the web. What are the consequences of these activities to reading and to background knowledge?

Reading Volume One change wrought by the digital revolution is that kids are actually reading much more than they used to, even though reading is commonly thought to be in decline. A 2009 study at the University

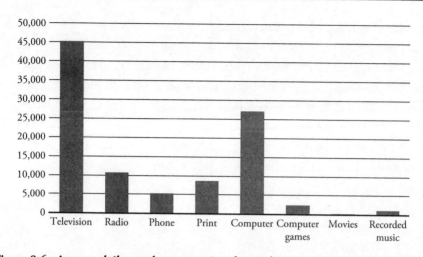

Figure 9.6. Average daily word consumption, by media. Note that the measure is "words," so they might be spoken, sung, or written.
Source: From "How much information?" by R. Bohn, J. Short, Global Information Industry Center, University of California, San Diego. Data from Appendix B, © UCSD (2009).

of California, San Diego, examined the number of words to which the average American is exposed per day (figure 9.6).

The volume of words received by computer is enormous. And although "by computer" includes words read and words heard, when the data were collected in 2008, most Americans did not have Internet access speed adequate for video or audio streaming. Most of the words they received would have been in print. These data were collected from adults, and are now half a decade old. Still, I think it's reasonable to suggest that kids do an enormous amount of incidental reading on digital platforms, especially in text messages, which this study did not include. So, does all this reading make them better readers?

We don't have firm data on this question, but reading theory would predict little benefit to comprehension from this type of material. Reading improves comprehension through the acquisition of broader background knowledge, but most of what the average kid reads on screens is not content rich. It's information within games, text messages, social network updates, and the like. But that sort of reading should (according to theory) have a positive effect on fluency. That prediction has not been tested as far as I know.

Knowledge Everywhere   Wait a minute. How can I be so sure that kids are not benefiting from this increase in reading? Doesn't it depend on *what* they are reading? You can read anything online, from a Shakespeare concordance to pornographic satire of *The Hunger Games* series.

Although we can say with wide-eyed innocence, "Hey, they *could* be reading Shakespeare," we suspect otherwise. One wag put it this way: "I possess a device, in my pocket, that is capable of accessing the entirety of information known to man. I use it to look at pictures of cats and get in arguments with strangers." Survey data confirm that teens use computers for a relatively limited number of activities. The most common are

- Social networking
- Playing games
- Watching videos
- Instant messaging

This survey is dated (it's from 1999), but at that time, these four activities accounted for *75 percent* of teens' computer time. Today instant messaging has been replaced by texting, to which the average teen devotes about ninety minutes daily. We can't generalize to every child, but I don't think it's the case that teen use of digital devices is so varied that we cannot make any claims about its likely impact.

Well, perhaps they are not seeking out rich sources of information but find themselves exposed to such information anyway. After all, the hallmark of the digital revolution is that it has made information cheap, in the best sense of the word. You can't help but get damp if you're in a flood, and the Internet is a fire hose of information.

Kids could learn in this incidental way, and there's evidence that they do, at least from certain sources. Toddlers and preschoolers who watch educational television really do learn about numbers and letters, as well as social lessons (e.g., about sharing). But overall, kids learn less from video than you'd think. Infants and toddlers seem to have a harder time learning from video than from a live person, a phenomenon established enough that it is called the "video deficit."

Mostly, the idea that new technologies leave people more knowledgeable goes unsupported. It might be right, but at the moment, it's unsupported. For older kids, the relationship between television viewing and academic achievement is negative, not positive; but note, that effect is carried by heavy viewers. Kids who watch only a little TV show no academic cost. (And for all kids, TV content, not just volume, matters.) More generally, kids who report being heavy users of all media (television, music, gaming, and the others) also report getting lower grades—but the relationship of grades and leisure reading is positive. Still, simple correlations like this don't tell us much about such complex behaviors.

Do We Need to Know Less?   Kids may not choose to read Shakespeare, but they could find information about his life or plays with ease. Those of us who grew up before the digital age truly find it miraculous that we can instantly find the name of the president during the War of 1812, whether jambalaya typically includes shellfish, or how to translate European shoe sizes to American. Whatever you want to know, however obscure, you can find it, and find it almost immediately.

Given the importance I placed in chapter 1 on knowledge as a driver of reading comprehension, we might ask whether easy access to information means that digital technologies render knowledge in one's head less important for reading (figure 9.7).

Figure 9.7. Marissa Mayer. In 2010 when she was vice president for search products and user experience at Google, Mayer wrote, "The Internet has relegated memorization of rote facts to mental exercise or enjoyment."[a] Mayer is now president and CEO of Yahoo!
Source: Photo © Yahoo. http://commons.wikimedia.org/wiki/File:Marissa_Mayer _May_2014_%28cropped%29.jpg.
[a]Mayer (2010).

There are three reasons that Googling information (or Yahooing it, or Binging it) is not a substitute for knowledge in your head when you are reading. First, if you recognize that you're missing something—you realize the writer has omitted some information that you need to make an inference—it's not always obvious which information is called for. Recall the example from chapter 1: "Trisha spilled her coffee. Dan jumped from his chair to get a rag." If you don't have the necessary knowledge in your head to understand why Dan jumped from his chair, you might search for "coffee" on the web. You're going to find an enormous amount of information: where coffee is grown, social customs around the world about how it's drunk, different ways to prepare it, and so on. That's a lot to sort through before you deduce which property the author assumed you knew.

A second problem with tracking down information is that you don't always know that you're missing anything. If that happens, it will likely be in the development of the situation model. I illustrated that point with the Carol Harris/Helen Keller story.

Finally, halting reading to find a definition or bit of information is disruptive. The more often you do it, the more likely you are to lose the logical thread of what you're reading and the more likely you are to quit reading it. So a substantial amount of knowledge needs to be known, not just findable.

When a Lack of Knowledge Hurts Comprehension

What can you do if you feel your child is not reading well because of a dearth of background knowledge? In the previous section, I argued that digital devices don't much improve knowledge and literacy, at least as kids usually employ them. The information superhighway may somewhere be roaring with frenetic power and speed, but your child has elected to dwell on familiar byways and cul-de-sacs. What other options are open if you feel your middle or high schooler lacks the broad background knowledge needed for effective reading comprehension?

Playing Knowledge Catch-Up   There's good news and bad news here. The good news is, as with fluency, that it's never too late. Sometimes you'll hear a news story about brain plasticity in early childhood that makes it sound as if there is a window of opportunity for learning in the early years that, if missed, means your child is out of luck. Not so. You can always learn. The bad news is that there is not a shortcut. Vocabulary and knowledge of the world accrete slowly, over the course of years. If there is an easy way to hurry it, scientists haven't found it.

And honestly, it's probably not useful to think of it as "catching up." You want your child to read more. Period. Yes, background knowledge helps, but that's in service of your child reading a wider variety of materials and enjoying them more. So meet him where he is, bearing in mind the big-picture goal. More reading, more fun. Not catching up.

Catching Up by Resetting the Starting Line   Your eighth grader might not be able to read a story written at an eighth-grade reading level, but the content and themes of books written for fourth graders will not be appealing. A possible solution is a book written to the tastes of older kids—the characters are their age, their relationship problems mirror theirs—but the books are written with simpler vocabulary and sentence structure. There are comparable nonfiction books. These books are called "hi-lo," short for "high interest, low reading level" (figure 9.8). (I list some publishers in the "Suggestions for Further Reading" section at the end of this book.)

Another approach is to find reading material on a subject that your child knows a lot about, thus circumventing the knowledge gap. A good choice is a book for which your child already knows the story. If he sees a movie he loves, see if it was based on a book or if a novelization has been published. If he loves a television show, a book of trivia and backstage gossip about the show might work. See if there is fan fiction written about a movie your child loves. (Fan fiction is a genre of new stories, written by fans, based on characters from an established television show, movie, or book. They are readily available on the web.) If your child is obsessed with an actor, find a biography. If it's a singer, find a book of song lyrics.

This reading material may strike you as trivial, but the goal is to get your child to think of leisure reading as a viable option. Thus, we're brushing up against the question of motivation. In the next chapter we'll tackle motivation in older kids head-on.

Figure 9.8. Hi-lo books. These books are so named because they contain high-interest content at a low reading level. The two books shown here are written at a third- or fourth-grade reading level but appeal to high schoolers. Note that the covers are meant to look age appropriate.

Keeping It Simple Summary

At School

- Limited time devoted to reading comprehension strategy instruction
- Beginning in middle school, increasing emphasis on domain-specific conventions about what to do with texts

At Home

- Don't try to help the child who lacks knowledge to "catch up." Help this child find ways to enjoy reading.

Notes

"That's especially true of poor readers, who are satisfied with a fairly minimal understanding of a text": Long, Oppy, and Seely (1994); Magliano and Millis (2003); Yuill, Oakhill, and Parkin (1989).

"It's not that they are unable to make appropriate inferences.": Johnston, Barnes, and Desrochers (2008).

"in one experiment, sixth graders were asked to read essays at the request of an experimenter": Markman (1979).

"studies show that teaching strategies improves reading comprehension": National Institute of Child Health and Human Development (2000).

"Just a few sessions—five or ten—give the same benefit as fifty.": Elbaum, Vaughn, Tejero Hughes, and Watson Moody (2000); Rosenshine, Meister, and Chapman (1996); Rosenshine and Meister (1994); Suggate (2010).

"they learn what merits special attention according to the conventions of the discipline": Shanahan and Shanahan (2008).

"differences, when they exist, are not due to limited learning abilities on the part of oldsters": Bennett, Maton, and Kervin (2008); Margaryan, Littlejohn, and Vojt (2011).

"when researchers at the University of Connecticut asked twenty-five seventh graders": Leu and Castek (2006).

"students rarely critically evaluate information they find on the web": Killi, Laurinen, and Marttunen (2008).

"but their evaluations of websites don't actually improve": Zhang and Duke (2011).

"examined the number of words to which the average American is exposed per day": Bohn and Short (2009).

" 'I use it to look at pictures of cats and get in arguments with strangers.' ": Nusername (2013).

"these four activities accounted for *75 percent* of teens' computer time": Rideout, Foehr, and Roberts (2010).

"preschoolers who watch educational television really do learn": D. R. Anderson et al. (2001); Ennemoser and Schneider (2007); Mares and Pan (2013).

"the 'video deficit'": Deocampo and Hudson (2005); Troseth, Saylor, and Archer (2006).

"TV content, not just volume, matters": For a review, see Guernsey (2007).

"but the relationship of grades and leisure reading is positive": Rideout et al. (2010).

10

The Reluctant Older Reader

I've already noted that reading motivation declines steadily as children age, reaching its lowest point by about grade 10. In this chapter, we consider strategies that teachers and parents might employ to arrest the slide.

What's Happening at School

In a nutshell, the problem of motivation is this: We want the child to do something we think is important but she chooses not to do it. That is, of course, a very common problem in classrooms. The typical motivator is punishment. A student who doesn't do the required work is punished by low grades, or perhaps the feeling of disappointing the teacher, or even feeling ashamed should the failure become public. But by the time a child is in middle school, these blades have long lost their edge. Most unmotivated readers have the self-assurance to persuade themselves that reading is not all that important. Schools are not enthusiastic about punishment in any event, so many turn to rewards as motivators.

Rewards

We want the child to read, and we want reading associated with a positive experience . . . well, what if I told a fourth grader, "If you read that book, I'll give you an ice cream sundae." The child might take me up on the deal, and it sounds like he'd have a positive experience. So won't he then then be motivated to read? It sounds so simple that it might be too good to be true (figure 10.1).

The Science of Rewards   Rewards do work, at least in the short term. If you find a reward that the child cares about, he will read in order to get it.

Figure 10.1. Book it button. Pizza Hut has conducted its Book It! program since 1984. Each month from October to March, if the child meets a reading target set by the teacher, he gets a certificate for a personal-size pizza. When he cashes in the certificate, the restaurant gives him a sticker to put on his Book It button. There are surprisingly few studies of the long-term impacts of the program on reading attitudes or habits. *Source:* Circa 1995 © Tim Stoops.

But what we're really concerned about is the reading attitude. When you stop giving the reward, will the attitude be more positive than when you began? Research indicates that the answer is often no. In fact, the attitude is often *less* positive because of the reward.

The classic experiment on this phenomenon was conducted in a preschool. A set of attractive markers appeared during free play, and the researchers affirmed that kids chose the markers from among many activities. Then the markers disappeared from the classroom. A few weeks later, researchers took kids, one at a time, into a separate room. They offered the child a fancy "good player" certificate if she would draw with the markers. Other kids were given the opportunity to draw with the markers but were not offered the certificate. A few weeks later, the markers reappeared during free play in the classroom. The kids who got the certificate showed notably less interest in the markers than the kids who didn't get the certificate. The reward had backfired: it had made kids like the markers less.

The interpretation of the study rests on how kids think about their own behavior. The rewarded kids likely thought, "I drew with the markers

Figure 10.2. The effects of rewards. Another example of how a reward changes your thinking about why you do something: people are often less likely to help a friend when offered a reward. If I ask you to help me move my couch, you probably perceive it as a social transaction; your reason to help me out is that you like to see yourself as helpful. But if I say, "I'll give you five dollars to help me move my couch," I've turned it into a financial transaction, and five dollars may not seem like enough money for the work.
Source: © Anne Murphy.
Note: For a readable review of these sorts of phenomena, see Ariely (2009, chap. 4).

because I was offered a reward to do so. Now here are the markers but no reward. So why would I draw with them?" There have been many studies of rewards in school contexts, and they often backfire in this way (figure 10.2).

We can imagine that rewarding kids for reading could work as intended in certain circumstances. What if the child has such a positive experience while reading that it overwhelms his thinking that he's reading only for the reward? In other words the child thinks, "Gosh, I started this book only to get that ice cream sundae, but actually it's awesome. My teacher was a sucker to offer me a sundae as a reward!" That's great when it does happen—and I think it can—but it means that rewards represent a risk. We're gambling that the book is going to be a big hit.

We might hope that a reward could do some good using another mechanism: that it would work like the bedtime-snuggle works—the child already likes ice cream (or whatever the reward is), and pairing it often enough with reading makes the good feeling of eating ice cream become associated with reading. The problem is that the child might consciously think, "I hate reading, but I like ice cream, so I guess I'll put up with reading." Researchers have examined whether that sort of conscious thought prevents the warm association from building, but the data are not clear.

What about praise instead of a reward? Generally praise is motivating to kids: they will do more of whatever was praised. But praise can go wrong if it's overly controlling ("I'm so glad to see you reading. You really should do that every day.") or if the child thinks it's dishonest ("You are the best reader at school."). But if the praise seems like sincere appreciation, it's motivating. And one of the advantages of praise is that it lacks the disadvantage of rewards. Rewards are usually set up in a bargain before the action: if you read, you'll get ice cream. Praise is generally spontaneous. You don't promise praise contingent on good behavior. That means that the praised child won't think, "I did that only to get the praise," the way that the rewarded child thinks, "I did that only to get the reward." The praised child elected to engage in the desired behavior of her own accord, and then the praise came spontaneously. The problem is that the child must choose to read on her own before you get a chance to praise her.

Rewards in Practice   As I'm sure is clear by now, I'm not a big fan of school-based rewards for reading. That includes public classroom displays of reading achievement—for example, posting on a bulletin board the number of books each student has read, or adding a segment of a class bookworm for each book. To my thinking, it puts too much emphasis on *having read* rather than on reading. Some students (I was one) will pick easy books to boost their "score." And as a way to recognize student achievement, it doesn't account for student differences; for some, getting through a book in a month may be a real achievement, yet they will feel inadequate compared to their peers. Some more formal programs (like Accelerated Reader* and Pizza Hut's Book It) try to make up for some of the problems inherent in a reward system. Different books are allocated different points based on difficulty, for example, or different students get different teacher-set reading targets.

---

*Accelerated Reader is software that allows for the tracking of individual students' reading. Books have different point values depending on length and difficulty, and students take brief quizzes to show that they've understood books they have read.

Still, I think it's a mistake to be so absolutist as to say rewards should never be used. Instead I'm suggesting they not be the first thing teachers try, and I want them to be aware of the research literature that describes the potential drawbacks. I know that some districts tune Accelerated Reader or another program to their own use, ignoring the points, for example. The research literature on Accelerated Reader in particular is, in fact, mixed. Much appears to depend on how it is implemented.

I'm also keeping in mind a conversation I had with a district administrator. Kids in her schools come from very poor homes, and she told me that they are not growing up seeing their parents read. A benefactor started a program whereby children earn cash for reading books, and the administrator felt that it was helpful. Kids had not been reading, the rewards got them started, and they discovered they really liked to read. I think it would be high-handed and naive to suggest that the district stop the program. In fact, this seems exactly the situation to try rewards: when you can't otherwise get a toehold, a way to get kids to at least *try* pleasure reading. The child may then discover that she likes it, and even when the rewards stop, she keeps going.

But if rewards are to be a last resort, as I'm suggesting, what ought to be tried first?

Pleasure Reading

Our goal is that children read because they feel the pleasure of reading; rewards were meant to be a temporary incentive to get the process going. Another way to frame the problem is this: kids are already feeling the pleasure of reading, but that feeling gets lost in less positive feelings—feelings created by the other demands of schoolwork.

Academic versus Pleasure Reading   We expect students to feel the joy of reading when they get lost in a narrative or feel the pleasure of discovery when reading nonfiction. But as I noted in chapter 9, this is the age at which we add other purposes to reading. One is learning: the student is expected to read a text and study it so that he can reproduce the information (e.g., on a quiz). A second purpose is to help complete a task—a project, say—and that usually entails gathering information. A third purpose is to analyze how a text works, that is, how the author writes to make the reader laugh or cry. I'll use the umbrella term *academic reading* to contrast these purposes with pleasure reading.

My concern is that kids might confuse academic reading with reading for pleasure. If they do, they will come to think of reading as work, plain and simple. Sure, we'd like to think that academic reading is pleasurable, but in most schools, "pleasure" is not a litmus test. The student who tells the teacher, "I tried reading that photosynthesis stuff, but it was too boring," will not be told to find something else she'd prefer. Academic reading feels like work because it *is* work. But pleasure ought to be the litmus test for reading for pleasure.

I think it's a good idea for teachers to communicate these distinctions to students—not that "most of the reading we're doing is academic, and therefore not fun," but that reading serves different purposes and that there is a distinction between academic reading and pleasure reading.

In some classrooms, pleasure reading *is* segregated from academic reading: we read because we love reading, and then we also learn how to work with texts. But the way that pleasure reading is handled can still send a silent message to students that reading is work. Coercion sends that message. I've warned against requirements that children read a set number of minutes per day at home or that a pleasurable activity be withheld until the child has completed his reading. The same goes for school. If a teacher makes pleasure reading a requirement (ten minutes per night, say) or demands accountability (by keeping a reading log, for example) students may think she believes that they would not read of their own accord.

Pleasure Reading in Class   I've said rewards shouldn't be off the table but also shouldn't be the first thing that schools try, and I've said coercion has drawbacks. What's left? I think the best strategy is the one that is successful at home: make reading expected and normal by devoting some proportion of class time to silent pleasure reading. A lot of what goes into a typical elementary reading program is not reading; in one study of six basal reading programs, researchers found that student reading averaged just fifteen minutes each day out of a reading block that averaged ninety minutes.

Successful programs for silent classroom reading tend to have certain elements in common:

- **Students need at least a twenty-minute reading period to get into their books.** Teachers set the duration dependent on the reading stamina of their students.
- **Students must freely choose what they read.** Choice is enormously important for motivation, but there must be teacher guidance and teacher-set limits. Given the chance, some students will pick books that entail no reading at all. (As researcher Nell Duke ruefully noted, "independent reading time" too often turns into "independent find Waldo time.") Teachers must not only monitor text difficulty, but also ensure that students are exposed to a variety of genres.
- **Students must have ready access to a good number of books** (figure 10.3).

Figure 10.3. Classroom library. Classroom libraries are highly desirable to facilitate silent pleasure reading. Unfortunately, classroom libraries become less common as kids advance through the grades.
Source: © LiMarie_AK via Flickr.

> - **Students should have some opportunity to feel a sense of community through reading** with book discussions, recommendations, and the other sorts of activities that avid adult readers practice.
> - **The teacher should be actively teaching during this time:** fielding questions, helping students select books, and conferring with students. The alternative is that the teacher reads her own book at the same time as the students, with the idea that she's modeling what a good reader does. But students can't see and appreciate what she's doing. Teachers teaching during reading time seems to be essential. Some of the most careful experiments indicate that without this feature, students don't benefit from silent reading time in class.

Setting aside time in the classroom for silent pleasure reading is the best solution I can see for a student who has no interest in reading. It offers the gentlest pressure that is still likely to work. Everyone else is reading, there's not much else to do, and a sharp-eyed teacher will notice those who are faking it. Freedom of choice also allows the greatest possibility that when the reluctant reader does give a book a try, he'll hit on something that he likes.

Given that I'm recommending this practice, you probably think there must be good research evidence that it boosts motivation. In truth, I'd say the latest data indicate that it *probably* improves attitudes, vocabulary, and comprehension. A lot of the research was not conducted in the best way, and the best experiments don't always support the practice.

I think the squishiness of the findings is attributable to the difficulty of the teaching method. I'm sure classroom pleasure reading is easy to implement poorly: stick some books in the room, allocate some class time, and you're done. But think of the teacher's responsibilities when it's done well. She must help students select books that they are likely to enjoy. That means really knowing each child, and a middle school teacher likely has more than one hundred students. If a teacher is going to be able to confer with students about what they have read, she needs to have read the book herself. Hence, she needs comprehensive knowledge of the literature appropriate to the grade level. And although I've said that silent pleasure reading is a good way to gently persuade reluctant students to give reading a try, let's not pretend this is easy. A sixth grader who believes that reading is boring has a pretty firm sense of herself as decidedly *not* a reader; a teacher must be a skilled psychologist to get around that attitude and get the student open to reading.

The skills and knowledge demanded of the teacher are one obstacle. A more serious one may be the attitude of some parents and administrators. If you walked into a sixth-grade classroom and saw the students sitting around reading novels, would you think that the teacher was kind of taking it easy? Would you think that the students were learning anything? Don't be that parent.

Other Features of Great Reading Classrooms

Silent pleasure reading is not a literacy program. If it's present at all, it will be just part of your child's day. If you visit your child's class, what else might you see as part of a classroom that will aid reading motivation?

Teachers who motivate readers are skilled in setting classroom activities that students find engaging and require reading if they are to be completed. Middle and high school students often hunger for school work that is less abstract and more related to their interests or to current events. It takes an inventive teacher to create lesson plans that account for this interest, *and* are rigorous, *and* meet school or district curriculum requirements. For example, I met a middle school science teacher who got his students interested in testing surface water quality in the neighborhood around the school. The students liked the possibility that their findings would have practical significance to the people living nearby, and it made them much more open to tackling challenging reading in science reference books.

Second, as in younger grades, teachers who motivate reading are those who avoid praising performance ("you read that really well") or student characteristics ("you're an excellent reader"). As with reward, praise offered for performance makes the student focus on performance and worry about errors, and ultimately it may lead him to choose work that will not stretch his abilities in order to ensure good performance that will earn praise. Better options are to praise a student for sticking with a difficult task or picking a book from a genre she had never tried before.

Third, teachers who motivate are not controlling. It's hard for students to be engaged when they know they have no voice in whatever comes next. Classrooms offer many opportunities for teachers to unwittingly control their students, for example, by talking too much, giving hyperdetailed instructions, interrupting students, or making decisions that seem arbitrary. In contrast, students are more likely to be motivated if their teacher listens to them, shows concern about student interests, acknowledges when work is challenging, and explains why work is being undertaken.

WHAT TO DO AT HOME

On the early side of this age range—the elementary years through middle school—much of what I've said in previous chapters about getting younger kids reading is still applicable, with some minor adjustments that I am guessing I don't need to spell out. But the challenge is different for middle and high schoolers. Compared to a nine-year-old, a fourteen-year-old has many more opportunities to avoid that home environment that you've tried to shape as a literary oasis, and they have a much stronger sense of themselves as "not a reader" or "a reader." In chapter 9 I mentioned that older children use more types of digital technologies. They also have greater access to them.

Are Gadgets Killing Reading?

Most of the parents I talk to are convinced that digital devices are having a profound and mostly negative impact on reading. The research on this issue is more limited than you might guess, because we're predicting a long-term consequence of the use of digital technologies and these technologies haven't been available that long. That said, I think the digital age *is* having a negative effect on motivation, but not through the mechanism that most parents fear.

Concentration Lost   A lot of teachers think that kids today are easily bored, and they blame digital devices for making them that way. Why are they to blame? Some observers—including prominent reading researcher

MaryAnn Wolf—have suggested that habitual web reading, characterized by caroming from one topic to another and skimming when they alight, changes the ability to read deeply. Nick Carr popularized this sinister possibility with the question: "Is Google Making Us Stoopid?" In that article (and in a follow-up book, *The Shallows*), Carr argued that something had happened to his brain. Years of quick pivots in his thinking prompted by web surfing had left him unable to read a serious novel or long article (figure 10.4). This does sound similar to the mental change many teachers feel they have seen in their students in the last decade or two; they can't pay attention, and teachers feel they must do a song and dance to engage them.

I doubt that reading on the web renders us unable to concentrate, and although a formal poll has not been taken, I suspect most cognitive psychologists are in my camp. Yes, video games and surfing the web change the brain. So does reading this book, singing a song, or seeing a stranger smile. The brain is adaptive, so it's always changing. If it's adaptive, couldn't that mean that it would adapt to the need for constant shifts in attention, and maybe thereby lose the ability to sustain attention to one thing? I don't

Figure 10.4. Does multitasking affect the brain? Trying to do two or things simultaneously demands frequent shifts in attention and could—the theory goes—exacerbate the web-generated tendency to read by skimming.
Source: © david goehring via Flickr.

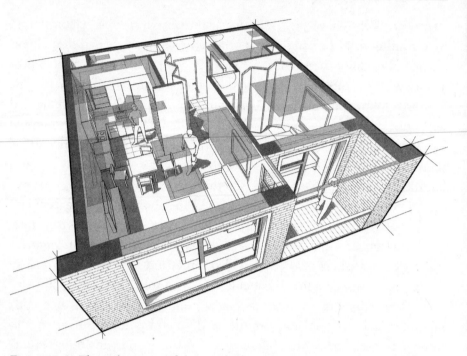

Figure 10.5. The architecture of the mind. The adaptability of the mind may be compared to a home's floor plan, where each room is like a cognitive process. You can expand or shrink rooms without affecting the overall design, but trying to move the living room from the front of the house to the back—a major reorganization—would be very disruptive.
Source: © Slavomir Valigursky—Fotolia.

think so, because the basic architecture of the mind probably can't be completely reshaped. Cognitive systems (vision, attention, memory, problem solving) are too interdependent for that. If one system changed in a fundamental way—such as losing the ability to stay focused on one object—that change would cascade through the entire cognitive system, affecting most or all aspects of thought. The brain is probably too conservative in its adaptability for that to happen (figure 10.5).

More important, I don't know of any good evidence that young people are worse at sustaining attention than their parents were at their age. Teens can sustain attention through a three-hour movie like *The Hobbit*. They are capable of reading a novel they enjoy like *The Perks of Being a Wallflower*. So I doubt that they can't sustain attention. But being able to sustain attention is no guarantee that they'll do so. They also have to deem something worthy of their attention, and that is where I think digital technologies may have their impact: they change expectations.

I'm Bored. Fix It   Despite the diversity of activities afforded by digital technologies, many do have two characteristics in common. First, whatever experience the technology offers, you get it immediately. Second, producing this experience requires minimal effort. For example, if you're watching a YouTube video and don't like it, you can switch to another. In fact, the website makes it simple by displaying a list of suggestions. If you get tired of videos, you can check Facebook. If that's boring, look for something funny on TheOnion.com. Watching television has the same feature: cable offers a few score of channels, but if nothing appeals, get something from Netflix (figure 10.6).

The consequence of long-term experience with digital technologies is not an inability to sustain attention. It's impatience with boredom. It's an expectation that I should always have something interesting to listen to,

Figure 10.6. Omnipresent entertainment. You have diversion in your pocket, so there is never a reason to be bored, even in the few minutes that these people are waiting for the Metro in the Washington, DC, area.
Source: © Jeffrey, via Flickr. https://www.flickr.com/photos/jb912/6483730553/in /photolist-aSWPcP-dqq4jD-fSELGZ-6DYhtp

watch, or read and that creating an interesting experience should require little effort. In chapter 4, I suggested that a child's choice to read should be seen in the context of what else she might do. The mind-boggling availability of experiences afforded by digital technologies means there is always something right at hand that one might do. Unless we're really engrossed, we have the continuous, nagging suspicion *there's a better way to spend my time than this.* That's why, when a friend sends a link to a video titled, "Dog goes crazy over sprinkler—FUNNY!" I find myself impatient if it's not funny within the first ten seconds. That's why my nephew asked me, "Why do I check my phone at red lights, even though I know I haven't received any important messages?" That's why teachers feel they must sing and dance to keep students' attention. We're not distractible. We just have a very low threshold for boredom.

If I'm right, there's good news; the distractibility we're all seeing is not due to long-term changes in the brain that represent a pernicious overhaul in how attention operates. It's due to beliefs—beliefs about what is worthy of sustained attention and about what brings rewarding experiences. Beliefs are difficult to change, true, but the prospect intimidates less than repairing a perhaps permanently damaged brain.

Some people focus less on cognitive changes wrought by digital technologies and more on behavior, specifically the raw amount of time they consume. How can one have time for anything else, including reading? Isn't it inevitable that people will read less if they devote more time to things other than reading?

The Displacements　　There's no time for reading! This idea is not new. It's called the displacement hypothesis, and though it comes in several varieties, the basic idea is that when a new activity (like browsing the web) becomes available, it takes the place of something else we have typically done (like reading). Evaluating whether that's true is tricky because lots of factors go into our choices. For example, if you simply ask the question, "Does television displace reading?" you're thinking that if it does, you'd expect a negative correlation: more TV goes with less reading, and less TV goes with more reading. But the wealthier you are, the more leisure time you have. So even if television does bite into reading time, we may not see the data pattern we expect because both activities are facilitated by free time.

So has reading been displaced by digital technologies? On balance, the answer seems to be no, although most of the research in this country has focused on adults, not children. Researchers have examined correlations between time spent on the Internet and time spent reading, statistically controlling for other variables like overall amount of leisure time as well as could be done. The correlation in most studies seems to be nil or slightly positive (in the direction opposite that predicted by the displacement hypothesis). Research on television viewing does indicate that heavy viewing (more than four hours each day) is associated with less reading.

Given the enormous amount of time devoted to digital technologies, how is it possible that they don't shove reading aside? One answer is that most people read so little there isn't much to be shoved aside. In 1999, when they had virtually no access to digital technologies (outside of gaming), children (ages eight to eighteen) spent an average of just twenty-one minutes per day reading books. In 2009, when access was much greater, they averaged twenty-five minutes. These data are a little deceptive, however, because they are averages. It's not that every child in 1999 read for about twenty-one minutes. Rather, some read quite a bit and some (about 50 percent) didn't read at all. So for half of kids, there was no chance for digital technologies to displace reading.

For the kids in 1999 who did read, it may be that reading provides a sort of pleasure that digital technologies don't replace. They like the fun that digital technologies provide, but it's a different sort of fun than they get from reading. Notably, magazine and newspaper reading did drop during the decade that followed, arguably because that sort of reading can be done on the Internet (figure 10.7).

So I'm offering a mixed message. Good news: I doubt digital activities are "changing kids' brains" in a scary way, and I don't think they soak up reading time. Bad news: I think they are leading kids to expect full-time amusement, and for some kids, reading time isn't soaked up only because there's little to soak up. It's already dry as a sun-bleached Saltine.

Positive Steps

The preceding section leads to a rather glum conclusion. But don't despair. There are positive steps you can take, even with a sulky teen, that might tempt him to read.

Figure 10.7. How television affected reading. When television became widely available in the 1950s, both reading and radio use dropped, but not across the board. People read less light fiction because television offered light drama. People saw television news coverage as thin, so they still read newspapers. This pattern of data led to the *functional equivalence* hypothesis: an activity is more likely to displace another if it better serves the same function. If it serves a different function, it's less likely to displace it.
Source: Wikimedia. http://commons.wikimedia.org/wiki/File:Family_watching_television_1958.jpg.

Shatter Reading Misconceptions   Danny Hoch has written and produced one-man performance pieces that have won two Obie awards. In an interview, he described one theater-goer's reaction to his one of his shows:

> This kid came to my show, like, "Yo, homeboy," with his hat to the side and his pants hanging off his ass. He came to my show four times and paid to get in, and he brought his friends, and I was blown away. He's like, "Hey, man, yeah, you know, I never seen anything like this. What is this?" And I said, "What do you mean, what is it?" And he said, "What do you call this that you're doing?" And I said, "Theater." And he said, "Nah. No, bullshit, it's not theater. What is it called?" And I said, "No, really, it's theater." And he said, "No, dude, if it was theater, it wouldn't be about me."

I think a lot of students have similar attitudes about reading. "Reading" means books written by dead people who have nothing to say that would be relevant to your life. Nevertheless, you are expected to pore over their words, study them, summarize them, analyze them for hidden meaning, and then write a five-page paper about them. That's reading. It's not contemporary. It doesn't have characters you can identify with. It's not nonfiction. It's not magazines or graphic novels.

What would your child find interesting? In chapter 9 I suggested you look for content with which your child is already familiar as a way of getting around a dearth of background knowledge. That makes sense from a motivational standpoint too, but if you are less worried about the knowledge angle, you might branch out by seeking a book with less familiar content but related to her interests. For example, my niece (along with millions of other teens) got interested in forensic science through the television show *CSI*.

When it comes to fiction, seek books that *look* fun. Remember that one factor that goes into the choices we make is an assessment of how likely we are to actually get the pleasure that the choice might afford. A thick book with small print looks intimidating to less-than-confident readers. Go for books that have short chapters or go for graphic novels, which look easy because of the pictures. (But be advised, many are challenging.) Kids in mid- to late-elementary school might appreciate a collection of a comic strip they enjoy. And older kids may be interested in manga (pronounced mayn-ga), a variety of comic from Japan. Manga are published in just about every genre you can think of: adventure, mystery, horror, fantasy, and comedy, but note, mature themes (sexuality, violence) are not rare (figure 10.8).

Another source to consider are websites like Wattpad and Inkpop. These operate a bit like social networking sites in that users "follow" people who post content. Users can also upvote content they like and comment on it. On these sites, the content is fiction. Amateur writers post stories, hoping to gain an audience. Much of the content is aimed at teens and preteens, and people often serialize their content; they don't post an entire novel, but rather post a chapter at a time. These bite-size portions might appeal to a reluctant reader—three thousand words is short enough to read on your phone during a bus ride.

Figure 10.8. Jeff Kinney, author of *Diary of a Wimpy Kid.* Kinney didn't intention-
ally write his books for reluctant readers, but the response from kids who previously
disliked reading has been overwhelming. Kinney's books are wonderfully written and
wonderfully funny, but the graphics are doubtless an important part of what makes them
inviting.
Source: Picture of Jeff Kinney reprinted with permission of the author.

It may be that none of this is to your taste. In fact, this sort of reading material may strike you as poorly written and as glorifying aspects of
popular culture that you find objectionable. That's a judgment call, of
course. I would not let my kids read material that is misogynistic, racist,
or the like. But if my teen avoided all reading, I would be fine with him
reading "junk." Before he can develop taste, he must experience hunger.
The first step is to open his mind to the idea that printed material is worth
his time. I believe parents will get further toward their own goals by showing curiosity about their children's interests rather than disdain for them.
Taking your child seriously as a reader—by, for example, taking a reading
recommendation from him—might make him take himself more seriously as a reader.

Get Help   Let's be realistic. Each time you hand your child a book
and he ends up hating it, he confirms to himself that reading is not
for him. Your efforts to persuade him to give reading a try (again) are
taxing for both of you, and it's not the kind of thing you're going to do

every day. So when you do try, you want it to be your best shot. Search "best books for reluctant teen readers" on the web and you'll find lots of lists. But you need something more fine-tuned to your child. You need someone with deep experience in the process of listening to a child's interests and tastes (his hobbies, the sort of music he likes, his personality, the subjects he likes and hates at school, the movies he enjoys), and then using that information to find a book maximally likely to intrigue him. Naturally, such a person must have an extensive knowledge of children's books.

There are two places you might find that sort of person: your school system and your public library. Librarians are a vastly underappreciated resource. They have wide knowledge of and passion for books, and are eager to help. You likely have an expert resource at your public library. Use it!

Finding the most knowledgeable person in your school or district may take a bit of tact. Your child's teacher is the obvious person to ask about your child's reading, and certainly you should. But there may be another teacher or reading coach who has made a real specialty of tempting reluctant readers. A suitable compromise might be to start with your child's teacher. If your gut tells you that her advice may not be enough, thank her and affirm that she's been helpful but also say that you're trying to gather as much information as you can, and you wonder whether there's anyone else she thinks is equally knowledgeable who might have some complementary ideas.

Use Social Connections   How does your child learn about movies he wants to see or video games he wants to play? Advertising. These media have huge budgets to make their product known. Kids also learn about the latest movie from friends—friends who learned about it from omnipresent advertising. Save a few highly successful series, there is *no* advertising for print material. It's all word of mouth, and most kids don't read.

You can try to correct this knowledge deficit directly by telling your teen about content you think she'd like. It probably won't produce an immediate turnaround, but it may plant a seed in her mind. More effective, though, would be for your child to hear these things from peers.

For adults, reading is often social. Part of the success of Oprah's book club is the feeling of being part of a group—maybe I wouldn't tackle *A Tale of Two Cities* on my own, but we're all in this together. Teens are hypersocial, so reading *ought* to be social for them as well.

If your child has friends who are readers, great. They are your best allies. More likely she doesn't, and it's possible that she is afraid (rightly or wrongly) that her nonreading friends think that reading is nerdy.* This is where technology can help. There are countless book groups on the web—boards where kids discuss books, trade recommendations, post fan fiction, and the like. (You can find examples in the "Suggestions for Further Reading" section at the end of this book.) Your child is not going to dive into one of these communities. The most likely entry point would be through that rare book that *does* capture her imagination; make sure she knows that there are websites where other enthusiasts discuss the book.

Make It Easy to Access Books   Will an electronic reader help motivation? There are a few scattered studies on this question, showing mixed results. Honestly, I'd be pretty surprised if an e-reader made books sexy to a child who hates reading. As we've noted, pleasure reading is not *that* different on an e-reader. Like their college counterparts, kids (ages nine to seventeen) prefer paper; 80 percent who have experience with e-books say they still read print more often.

Yet these same kids say they think they would read more if they had access to e-books, and I tend to believe them. I don't think e-readers make reading more fun, once the device has lost its gee-whiz luster. But an e-reader improves access. Being able to download virtually any book you want as soon as you want it (barring cost considerations) is a great advantage. If your child has just finished book two of a trilogy or he's just heard from a friend about a fantastic new title, *that's* when he's most excited about

---

*I once saw a boy who looked to be about eleven years old reading by a swimming pool. Another kid popped out of the water and said, "What are you *reading* for? That's so boring!" The first boy looked up and said with cool disdain, "It's good for your brain." I wanted to hug him but restrained myself.

getting it. But if he has to wait a few days to get to a bookstore or library, his interest may have moved on to something new. Older kids can download an e-reader for their phone. It's free, and that way they can always have a book with them.

Help Your Child with Scheduling   Some teens like the idea of reading but simply cannot find the time. Activities today do seem much more intense than they were a generation ago; something as seemingly simple as playing soccer or singing in the choir calls for many hours each week. Add in homework, and kids feel that their week is overflowing. How can you help a child who likes the idea of reading find time to do so?

It may not be that your child has no time, but rather that she doesn't have large blocks of it. She may believe that reading must occur in silence and for some minimum duration. If her teacher says, "Try to read for thirty minutes each night," it's easy to see why a student would assume that means thirty consecutive minutes. But adult readers find crumbs of time throughout the day to feed their reading hunger. Your child may simply need to get used to keeping a book with her, to be read in snippets: on the school bus, waiting for a parent to pick her up from her piano lesson, in a long line at McDonald's. How about an audiobook for her iPod on the ride to school? I like to ask students if they have been bored at any time in the last month. If so, that's a time they could have been reading.

You might also introduce students to a common strategy we adults use when we're short of time: we schedule it. You can't simply hope to find time to do important things—you must make time to do them, and that's done by consciously selecting a specific time and place that you'll read. Equally important, your child should anticipate why he wouldn't read at that planned time. If he plans to read for fifteen minutes at 5:00 p.m. each evening, what might make him decide at that time that he ought to skip reading that day? Or what might interrupt him once he starts? He needs to plan strategies to deal with those interruptions. If he skips reading because he feels panicky about his homework, maybe reading time needs to be rescheduled. If he's frequently interrupted by his little brother, maybe he needs to choose a more private place to read.

Keeping It Simple Summary

At School

- A distinction drawn between academic reading and pleasure reading
- Rewards and coercion used as a last resort
- Pleasure reading in classrooms, coupled with instruction during these sessions

At Home

- Don't nag, praise, criticize content, or otherwise control your child's reading.
- Seek ways to involve your child in a peer network of readers.
- Make it easy to access books.
- Help your child find a good time and place to read.

NOTES

"The classic experiment on this phenomenon was conducted in a preschool.": Lepper, Greene, and Nisbett (1973).

"There have been many studies of rewards in school contexts, and they often backfire in this way": For a review, see Deci, Koestner, and Ryan (1999).

"What about praise instead of a reward?": For a review of praise, see Willingham (2005).

"The research literature on Accelerated Reader in particular is, in fact, mixed.": Hansen, Collins, and Warschauer (2009).

"My concern is that kids might confuse academic reading with reading for pleasure.": For a thorough treatment, see Gallagher (2009).

"just fifteen minutes each day out of a reading block that averaged ninety minutes": Brenner, Hiebert, and Tompkins (2009).

"As researcher Nell Duke ruefully noted": Miller and Moss (2013).

"as kids advance through the grades": Fractor, Woodruff, Martinez, and Teale (1993).

"Some of the most careful experiments indicate that without this feature, students don't benefit from silent reading time in class.": Kamil (2008).

"I'd say the latest data indicate that it *probably* improves attitudes, vocabulary, and comprehension": Manning and Lewis (2010); Yoon (2002).

"A lot of teachers think that kids today are easily bored, and they blame digital devices for making them that way.": Richtel (2012).

"prominent reading researcher MaryAnn Wolf": Rosenwald (2014).

"'Is Google Making Us Stoopid?'": Carr (2008).

"follow-up book, *The Shallows*": Carr (2011).

"I suspect most cognitive psychologists are in my camp": Steven Pinker and Roger Schank have both written in this vein: http://edge.org/q2010/q10_10.html#pinker;%20http://www.edge.org/q2010/q10_13.html. See also Mills (2014).

"say they still read print more often": Robinson (2014).

CONCLUSION

As I neared the completion of this book I asked some friends to read what I had written. Several made the same comment, saying something like, "This is all interesting, but one thing you haven't said is that some kids are just destined not to be readers. And you don't want those kids to feel bad, to feel like they are out of step with the family value of reading. So if you had a child like that, you'd back off, right?"

No, I wouldn't.

Why might a child feel pressured about reading? An obvious answer is that reading does not come easily to him. He'd rather opt out, especially if he compares himself to siblings who seem to read effortlessly. But reading can still bring pleasure, even if it's a little tougher to obtain. Every child should be met where he is and get the pleasures available from what he can do. My family doesn't refrain from taking walks because one of us is confined to a wheelchair. My daughter can't hike a mountain trail or walk a sandy beach, but she "walks" as she can and enjoys what's available. I think backing off is exactly the wrong message. Doing so says, "I indicated before that reading is important, but now that I see you're having trouble, let's pretend it's not." The child won't be fooled. The child will conclude that the problem is too terrible to be openly discussed.

Rather than deny, I prefer to normalize. It's normal that some things come more easily to one child than to her sibling. Why not be frank and say, "Yes, this is difficult for you, I can see. I'm impressed by how hard you're working at it"? The thing is, every child has a turn learning something that comes easily and learning something else that doesn't. Maybe it's math, or it's being brave enough to take a bus downtown alone, or it's learning to ride a bike, or it's telling a friend that she's let you down. I want my children to be gracious when things come easily and determined when they don't. I'm not going to implicitly suggest they abandon things I believe are important when the going gets tough.

But for other kids, the issue is not that they have trouble reading; it's that they just don't seem very interested. I realize that what I've written in these chapters could easily be taken as a setup for your child to feel pressured to enjoy reading because this book has offered a whole lot of "do this, do that, for heaven's sake don't do this other thing." The reason I've been so directive is that stating the objectives is not enough. I can't just say, "The goal is for your child to love reading. Now go forth and do good." I had to discuss the specifics of how that goal plays out day to day and what to do about the obstacles that are likely to arise. But too great a focus on the detailed instructions can lead to nearsightedness and, ultimately, mistakes (figure C.1).

You avoid myopia by reminding yourself to look up from the details every now and then to gain perspective—in other words, remind yourself of your ultimate goal. In the Introduction, I noted that I wasn't much interested in getting my kids to read because leisure reading is associated with success in school or earning more money. My desire for my children to read is simply a gut instinct. Here at the book's close, I think I can amplify on that. What I really want is for my children to experience reading pleasure.

Figure C.1. Taking instructions too literally. This may be an urban myth, but the story is that a woman ordered a birthday cake and told the clerk she wanted these words on it: "Happy Birthday, and under that, All the best wishes." The decorator dutifully wrote exactly what was described. You have to keep the overall goal of a project in mind, not just faithfully comply with the instructions.

What sort of reading pleasure? For me, reading affords a pleasure of understanding. Food writer Ruth Reichl can snare in words the elusive subtleties in the flavor of toro. Other writers make me understand things about myself, not always appealing things. After reading the memoir *Clear Pictures*, I remember reflecting on how lucky Reynolds Price was to have grown up among such wise and interesting people, only to realize that it was Price's acumen and sensitivity that made them so; had I known them, I would likely have missed their finest qualities. As an adult, I get great satisfaction from at long last coming to a better understanding of ideas that I've long encountered but only dimly comprehended; most recently, it's been the tensions among the founders of the United States.

An altogether different sort of pleasure comes from being carried to distant times and places when I read. How better to see the French Riviera during the 1920s than through the debauched, exhausted eyes of Dick Diver in *Tender Is the Night*? How could I enter the alternately solemn and boisterous world of New York's Hasidim if Chaim Potok did not take me there? And then too, sometimes the pleasure lies not in the charms of a new world but in escape from my own. During graduate school, I read Herman Wouk's two-volume World War II epic, *Winds of War* and *War and Remembrance*, nearly daily at lunch; I used it like worry beads to manage the anxiety consequent to my demanding academic program.

I maintain that these joys cannot be experienced through television or other media. Only reading elicits *your* contribution to the experience by demanding that you mentally create the world described. Only fiction demands that you live with the characters as long or as deeply. And with few exceptions, prose stylists show greater love of language than artists in other media.

I want my children and yours to experience those joys, or ones like them. And that's where you must keep the goal in the forefront of your mind. As someone who has spent all of his professional life around eighteen- to twenty-two-year-olds, I'll offer my impression as to what causes the greatest conflict between parents and teens. Parents are under the impression that they want their child to be happy. Children are under the impression that their parents want them to be happy the way their parents think they ought to be happy.

That's where the danger lies in a child feeling pressured and unhappy about reading. Remember that your goal is that your kids enjoy reading, not that they enjoy reading as you do. For you, it may be literary fiction. For your child, it may be the contemplative precision of poetry, or the muscular plotting of the thriller, or the funhouse distortions of horror. Or perhaps your children will show you the pleasure to be had from *Geocacher Magazine* or compendia of technical motorcycle engine diagrams. Let your child enjoy and explore the pleasure of reading as he can. And if it helps you, periodically look up from day-to-day life, and recall the principles I suggested at this book's outset: we start now, and we have fun.

Have fun.

APPENDIX

ACCESSING THE BONUS WEB CONTENT

In a perfect world, a child's caregiver and teachers are equally committed to helping the child develop a love of reading. But in some cases a teacher must shoulder most or all of the work—for instance, when parents are juggling multiple jobs or have difficulty reading themselves.

What can teachers do when parent participation is not a sure thing? To access bonus material from Dan Willingham on this topic, go to the publisher's website at www.wiley.com/go/kidsread and use the password **69720**.

SUGGESTIONS FOR FURTHER READING

READABLE REVIEWS OF THE SCIENTIFIC LITERATURE ON READING

Dehaene, S. (2009). *Reading in the Brain*. New York: Viking. A fairly high-level trade book, using a neuroscientific perspective.

Kamil, M. L., Pearson, P. D., Moje, E. B., & Afflerbach, P. P. (2011). *Handbook of Reading Research* (vol. 4). New York: Routledge. A huge volume with chapters on many topics written by leading researchers. It's meant to be read by other researchers, so it's far from a beginner's guide, but if you want the straight research dope, it's an amazing resource.

Samuels, S. J., & Farstrup, A. E. (2011). *What Research Has to Say about Reading Instruction* (4th ed.). Newark, DE: International Reading Association. Another edited volume with contributions from many top reading researchers.

Wasik, B. H. (2012). *Handbook of Family Literacy* (2nd ed.). New York: Routledge. Because it's concerned with literacy more broadly, this book offers chapters on a wider variety of topics, including mathematical literacy and global perspectives on literacy.

RESOURCES ABOUT RAISING A READER

Cunningham, A., & Zibulsky, J. (2014). *Book Smart*. New York: Oxford University Press. Similar in spirit to this book, but with more detail on research.

Institute of Education Sciences practice guides: http://1.usa.gov/1fUvsep. A wonderful, underused resource. These are free, downloadable documents, varying in length, written by expert panels on evidence-based practice. Each guide covers one topic, usually specified by age and content (e.g., "Teaching elementary school children to write").

ReadingRockets.com: wonderful website with resources for parents and teachers.

Dyslexia

Shaywitz, S. (2003). *Overcoming Dyslexia*. New York: Random House. Sally Shaywitz is a leading researcher in the field, and this book, although a decade old, is a very readable, practical summary of what's known and what to do.

Three websites are excellent resources for up-to-date information about cutting-edge research, as well as passing fads:

International Dyslexia Association: http://www.interdys.org/

National Institutes of Health: http://www.ninds.nih.gov/disorders /dyslexia/dyslexia.htm

Yale Center for Dyslexia and Creativity: http://dyslexia.yale.edu/

Choosing Books

Goodreads: http://www.goodreads.com/genres/childrens. A social networking website for readers with more than 10 million members. Users can write and read reviews among many other functions, and if you "like" books, new titles will be recommended to you.

Hearne, B., & Stevenson, D. (2000). *Choosing books for children: A commonsense guide* (3rd ed.). Champaign: University of Illinois Press. Chapters organized by age and topic, each starting with observations about the genre and general advice about book selection within it, then moving on to specific recommendations.

Lipson, E. R. (2000). *The New York Times Parent's Guide to the Best Books for Children* (3rd ed.). New York: Random House. Over five hundred pages of book recommendations with brief descriptions, broadly categorized by age.

National Education Association's "Teachers' Top 100 Books for Children," http://www.nea.org/grants/teachers-top-100-books-for-children.html. Based on a one-time survey conducted in 2007 and just a single list for all ages. Still, it's interesting to see what teachers think of as great books for kids.

Oprah's Reading List for Kids. Oprah.com has a number of reading suggestions for kids, including lists organized by age and by the child's interests.

Read Aloud America: http://www.readaloudamerica.org/booklist.htm. A nonprofit devoted to literacy, lifetime reading, and especially read-alouds. The website offers recommendations finely tuned to age, but no descriptions.

Trelease, J. (2013). *The Read-Aloud Handbook* (7th ed.). New York: Penguin. A classic. Trelease gives advice about how to read aloud and offers about 150 pages of suggestions. The accompanying descriptions are brilliantly clear and brief, so that, more than for other lists, you get some flavor of the book. The claimed benefits of reading aloud are a little overhyped, but it's hard to get snippy with such an eloquent advocate of read-alouds.

Social Networks for Teen Readers

Amazon: http://www.amazon.com/forum/book: If you've been to Amazon .com (and who hasn't?) you're familiar with the book reviews. There are also discussions, separate from the reviews. Popular books have lively discussions, and because everyone knows about Amazon, they are often heavily populated.

Goodreads: http://www.goodreads.com/genres/young-adult: Like Amazon, this site is meant for all readers, not just teens, and like Amazon, users can comment on other people's posts and "like" them. Goodreads also allows the posting of pictures and animated GIFs, which teens do in abundance. It gives the young adult section a much more teen-oriented sensibility.

readergirlz.com, guyslitwire.com, teenreads.com: These three websites are written by and for people who are already serious readers; each relishes its persona of slight nerdiness. They offer reviews, a blog, author interviews, and so on. They might be a welcome home for teens who like reading but don't have friends who do.

Hi-Lo Publishers

The following publishers have good Hi-Lo lists. You can also search for "hi-lo books" or "hi-lo publishers" on the web:

Capstone: http://www.capstoneclassroom.com/content/home_hilo

High Noon: http://www.highnoonbooks.com/index-hnb.tpl

Orca: http://us.orcabook.com/catalog.cfm?CatPos=373

Perfection Learning: http://www.perfectionlearning.com/browse
.php?categoryID=3929

Saddleback: http://www.sdlback.com/hi-lo-reading

WORKS CITED

Ackerman, R., & Goldsmith, M. (2011). Metacognitive regulation of text learning: On screen versus on paper. *Journal of Experimental Psychology: Applied, 17*(1), 18–32. doi:10.1037/a0022086

Ackerman, R., & Lauterman, T. (2012). Taking reading comprehension exams on screen or on paper? A metacognitive analysis of learning texts under time pressure. *Computers in Human Behavior, 28*(5), 1816–1828. doi:10.1016/j.chb.2012.04.023

Anderson, D. R., Huston, A. C., Schmitt, K. L., Linebarger, D. L., Wright, J. C., & Larson, R. (2001). Childhood television viewing and adolescent behavior: The recontact study. *Monographs of the Society for Research in Child Development, 66*(1), 1–154.

Anderson, R. C. (1985). *Becoming a nation of readers: The Report of the Commission on Reading.* Retrieved from http://files.eric.ed.gov/fulltext/ED253865.pdf.

Anderson, R. C., Wilson, P. T., & Fielding, L. G. (1988). Growth in reading and how children spend their time outside of school. *Reading Research Quarterly, 23*(3), 285–303.

Anthony, J. L., & Francis, D. J. (2005). Development of phonological awareness. *Current Directions in Psychological Science, 14*(5), 255–259. doi:10.1111/j.0963-7214.2005.00376.x

Arciuli, J., & Simpson, I. C. (2012). Statistical learning is related to reading ability in children and adults. *Cognitive Science, 36*(2), 286–304. doi:10.1111/j.1551-6709.2011.01200.x

Ariely, D. (2009). *Predictably irrational.* New York: HarperCollins.

Arnold, D. S., & Whitehurst, G. J. (1994). Accelerating language development through picture book reading: A summary of dialogic reading and its effect. In D. K. Dickenson (Ed.), *Bridges to literacy: Children, families and schools* (pp. 103–128). Malden, MA: Blackwell.

Aronson, E., Wilson, T. D., & Akert, R. M. (2012). *Social Psychology* (8th ed.). New York: Pearson.

Backman, J. (1983). The role of psycholinguistic skills in reading acquisition: A look at early readers. *Reading Research Quarterly, 18*(4), 466–479.

Baker, L. (2003). The role of parents in motivating struggling readers. *Reading and Writing Quarterly: Overcoming Learning Difficulties, 19*(1), 87–106.

Baker, L., & Scher, D. (2002). Beginning readers' motivation for reading in relation to parental beliefs and home reading experiences. *Reading Psychology, 23,* 239–269.

Baker, L., Scher, D., & Mackler, K. (1997). Home and family influences on motivations for reading. *Educational Psychologist, 32*(2), 69–82.

Banilower, E. R., Smith, P. S., Weiss, I. R., Malzahn, K. A., Campbell, K. M., & Weis, A. M. (2013). *Report of the 2012 national survey of science and mathematics education.* Chapel Hill, NC: Horizon Research, Inc.

Barclay, J. R., Bransford, J. D., Franks, J. J., McCarrell, N. S., & Nitsch, K. (1974). Comprehension and semantic flexibility. *Journal of Verbal Learning and Verbal Behavior, 13*(4), 471–481. doi:10.1016/S0022–5371(74)80024–1

Bennett, S., Maton, K., & Kervin, L. (2008). The "digital natives" debate: A critical review of the evidence. *British Journal of Educational Technology, 39*(5), 775–786. doi:10.1111/j.1467–8535.2007.00793.x

Bennett, S. E., Rhine, S. L., & Flickinger, R. S. (2000). Readings impact on democractic citizenship in America. *Political Behavior, 22*(3), 167–195.

Bingham, G. E., & Hall-Kenyon, K. M. (2013). Examining teachers' beliefs about and implementation of a balanced literacy framework. *Journal of Research in Reading, 36*(1), 14–28. doi: 10.1111/j.1467–9817.2010.01483.x

Bohn, R. E., & Short, J. E. (2009). *How much information? 2009 report on American consumers.* San Diego: Global Information Industry Center, University of California, San Diego. Retrieved from http://hmi.ucsd.edu/howmuchinfo.php

Bottomley, D. M., Truscott, D. M., Marinak, B. A., Henk, W. A., & Melnick, S. A. (1999). An affective comparison of whole language, literature-based, and basal reader literacy instruction. *Reading Research and Instruction, 38*(2), 115–129. doi:10.1080/19388079909558282

Braten, I., Lie, A., Andreassen, R., & Olaussen, B. S. (1999). Leisure time reading and orthographic processes in word recognition among Norwegian third- and fourth-grade students. *Reading and Writing, 11,* 65–88.

Brenner, D., Hiebert, E. H., & Tompkins, R. (2009). How much and what are third graders reading? In E. H. Hiebert (Ed.), *Reading more, reading better* (pp. 118–140). New York: Guilford Press.

Breznitz, Z., & Share, D. L. (1992). Effects of accelerated reading rate on memory for text. *Journal of Educational Psychology, 84*(2), 193–199.

Card, D. (1999). The causal effect of education on earnings. *Handbook of Labor Economics, 3,* 1801–1863. doi:10.1016/S1573-4463(99)03011-4

Carlson, K. (2009). How prosody influences sentence comprehension. *Language and Linguistics Compass, 3*(5), 1188–1200. doi:10.1111/j.1749-818X.2009.00150.x

Carr, N. (2008). Is Google making us stoopid? *Yearbook of the National Society for the Study of Education, 107*(2), 89–94. doi:10.1111/j.1744-7984.2008.00172.x

Carr, N. (2011). *The shallows: What the Internet is doing to our brains.* New York: Norton.

Carver, R. (1994). Percentage of unknown vocabulary words in text as a function of the relative difficulty of the text: Implications for instruction. *Journal of Literacy Research, 26*(4), 413–437. doi:10.1080/10862969409547861

Chall, J. (1967). *Learning to read: The great debate.* New York: McGraw-Hill.

Cheung, A.C.K., & Slavin, R. E. (2011, May). The effectiveness of education technology for enhancing reading achievement: A meta-analysis. 1–48. The Center for Research and Reform in Education, Johns Hopkins University. Retrieved from http://www.bestevidence.org/reading/tech/tech.html.

Chouinard, M. M., Harris, P. L., & Maratsos, M. P. (2007). Children's questions: A mechanism for cognitive development. *Monographs of the Society for Research in Child Development, 72*(1), 1–129. Retrieved from http://www.jstor.org/stable/30163594.

Claessens, A., Engel, M., & Curran, F. C. (2013). Academic content, student learning, and the persistence of preschool effects. *American Educational Research Journal, 51*, 403–434.

Clark, C., & DeZoysa, S. (2011). *Mapping the interrelationships of reading enjoyment, attitudes, behaviour and attainment: An exploratory investigation.* London. Retrieved from http://files.eric.ed.gov/fulltext /ED541404.pdf.

Collins, W. M., & Levy, B. A. (2008). Developing fluent text processing with practice: Memorial influences on fluency and comprehension. *Canadian Psychology/Psychologie Canadienne, 49*(2), 133–139. doi: 10.1037/0708–5591.49.2.133

Connell, C., Bayliss, L., & Farmer, W. (2012). Effects of eBook readers and tablet computers on reading comprehension. *International Journal of Instructional Media, 39*(2), 131–141.

Connor, C. M., Morrison, F. J., & Katch, L. E. (2004). Beyond the reading wars: Exploring the effect of child-instruction interactions on growth in early reading. *Scientific Studies of Reading, 8*(4), 305–336.

Connor, C. M., Morrison, F. J., & Petrella, J. N. (2004). Effective reading comprehension instruction: Examining Child × Instruction interactions. *Journal of Educational Psychology, 96*(4), 682–698.

Cunningham, A. E., & Stanovich, K. E. (1991). Tracking the unique effects of print exposure in children: Associations with vocabulary, general knowledge, and spelling. *Journal of Educational Psychology, 83*(2), 264–274. doi:10.1037//0022–0663.83.2.264

Cunningham, A. E., & Stanovich, K. E. (1997). Early reading acquisition and its relation to reading experience and ability 10 years later. *Developmental Psychology, 33*(6), 934–945.

Daane, M. C., Campbell, J. R., Grigg, W. S., Goodman, M. J., & Oranje, A. (2005). *Fourth-grade students reading aloud: NAEP 2002 Special Study of Oral Reading.* Washington, DC: National Center for

Education Statistics. Retrieved from https://nces.ed.gov/pubsearch/pubsinfo.asp?pubid=2006469.

Daniel, D. B., & Willingham, D. T. (2012). Electronic textbooks: Why the rush? *Science, 335,* 1569–1571.

Daniel, D. B., & Woody, W. D. (2013). E-textbooks at what cost? Performance and use of electronic v. print texts. *Computers and Education, 62,* 18–23. doi:10.1016/j.compedu.2012.10.016

de Jong, M. T., & Bus, A. G. (2002). Quality of book-reading matters for emergent readers: An experiment with the same book in a regular or electronic format. *Journal of Educational Psychology, 94*(1), 145–155. doi:10.1037//0022–0663.94.1.145

de Jong, M. T., & Bus, A. G. (2004). The efficacy of electronic books in fostering kindergarten children's emergent story understanding. *Reading Research Quarterly, 39,* 378–393.

DeBaryshe, B. D. (1995). Maternal belief systems: Linchpin in the home reading process. *Journal of Applied Developmental Psychology, 16*(1), 1–20. doi:10.1016/0193–3973(95)90013–6

Deci, E. L., Koestner, R., & Ryan, R. M. (1999). A meta-analytic review of experiments examining the effects of extrinsic rewards on intrinsic motivation. *Psychological Bulletin, 125*(6), 627–668. Retrieved from http://psycnet.apa.orgjournals/bul/125/6/627.

Deocampo, J. A., & Hudson, J. A. (2005). When seeing is not believing: Two-year-olds' use of video representations to find a hidden toy. *Journal of Cognition and Development, 6*(2), 229–258. doi:10.1207/s15327647jcd0602_4

DeStefano, D., & LeFevre, J.-A. (2007). Cognitive load in hypertext reading: A review. *Computers in Human Behavior, 23*(3), 1616–1641. doi:10.1016/j.chb.2005.08.012

Dickinson, D. K., Golinkoff, R. M., & Hirsh-Pasek, K. (2010). Speaking out for language: Why language is central to reading development. *Educational Researcher, 39*(4), 305–310. doi:10.3102/0013189X10370204

Dowhower, S. L. (1989). Repeated reading: Research into practice. *Reading Teacher, 42,* 389–406.

Duke, N. K. (2000). 3.6 minutes per day: The scarcity of informational texts in first grade. *Reading Research Quarterly, 35*(2), 202–224. doi:10.1598/RRQ.35.2.1

Eccles, J., Wigfield, A., Harold, R. D., Blumenfeld, P., & Url, S. (1993). Age and gender differences in children's self- and task perceptions during elementary school. *Child Development, 64*(3), 830–847.

Ehri, L. C. (2008). Development of sight word reading: Phases and findings. In M. J. Snowling & C. Hulme (Eds.), *The science of reading: A handbook* (pp. 135–154). Oxford, UK: Blackwell.

Elbaum, B., Vaughn, S., Tejero Hughes, M., & Watson Moody, S. (2000). How effective are one-to-one tutoring programs in reading for elementary students at risk for reading failure? A meta-analysis of the intervention research. *Journal of Educational Psychology, 92*(4), 605–619. doi:10.1037//0022–0663.92.4.605

Ennemoser, M., & Schneider, W. (2007). Relations of television viewing and reading: Findings from a four-year longitudinal study. *Journal of Educational Psychology, 99*(2), 349–368. doi:10.1037/0022–0663.99.2.349

EU High Level Group of Experts on Literacy. (2012). *Final report.* Luxembourg. Retrieved from http://ec.europa.eu/education/policy/school/doc/literacy-report_en.pdf.

Evans, M. A., Shaw, D., & Bell, M. (2000). Home literacy activities and their influence on early literacy skills. *Canadian Journal of Experimental Psychology/Revue Canadienne de Psychologie Expérimentale, 54*(2), 65–75. Retrieved from http://www.ncbi.nlm.nih.gov/pubmed/10881391.

Fleisher, L. S., Jenkins, J. R., & Pany, D. (1979). Effects on poor readers' comprehension of training in rapid decoding. *Reading Research Quarterly, 15*(1), 30–48.

Foertsch, J., & Gernsbacher, M. A. (1994). In search of complete comprehension: Getting "minimalists" to work. *Discourse Processes, 18*(3), 271–296. doi:10.1080/01638539409544896

Fountas, I. C., & Pinnell, G. S. (1996). *Guided reading: Good first teaching for all children.* Portsmouth, NH: Heinemann.

Fractor, J. S., Woodruff, M. C., Martinez, M. G., & Teale, W. H. (1993). Let's not miss opportunities to promote voluntary reading: Classroom libraries in the elementary school. *Reading Teacher*, *46*, 476–484.

Gallagher, K. (2009). *Readicide*. Portland, ME: Stenhouse.

Goodman, K. (1996). *On reading: A common-sense look at the nature of language and the science of reading*. Portsmouth, NH: Heinemann.

Grainger, J., Lété, B., Bertand, D., Dufau, S., & Ziegler, J. C. (2012). Evidence for multiple routes in learning to read. *Cognition*, *123*(2), 280–92. doi:10.1016/j.cognition.2012.01.003

Grotevant, H. D. (1987). Toward a process model of identity formation. *Journal of Adolescent Research*, *2*(3), 203–222. doi:10. 1177/074355488723003

Guernsey, L. (2007). *Into the minds of babes: How screen time affects children from birth to age five*. New York: Basic Books.

Guthrie, J. T., & Cox, K. E. (2001). Classroom conditions for motivation and engagement in reading. *Educational Psychology Review*, *13*(3), 283–302. doi:10.1023/A:1016627907001

Haidt, J. (2012). *The righteous mind: How good people are divided by politics and religion*. New York: Random House.

Hall, L. A. (2012). Rewriting identities: Creating spaces for students and teachers to challenge the norms of what it means to be a reader in school. *Journal of Adolescent and Adult Literacy*, *55*(5), 368–373. doi:10.1002/JAAL.00045

Hansen, L. E., Collins, P., & Warschauer, M. (2009). Reading management programs: A review of the research. *Journal of Literacy and Technology*, *10*(3), 56–80.

Harter, S. (1999). *The cognitive and social construction of the developing self*. New York: Guilford Press.

Hattie, J. (2009). *Visible learning*. London: Routledge.

Holden, M. H., & MacGinitie, W. H. (1972). Children's conceptions of word boundaries in speech and print. *Journal of Educational Psychology*, *63*(6), 551–557. Retrieved from http://psycnet.apa.orgjournals /edu/63/6/551.

Hood, M., Conlon, E., & Andrews, G. (2008). Preschool home literacy practices and children's literacy development: A longitudinal analysis. *Journal of Educational Psychology, 100*(2), 252–271. doi: 10.1037/0022–0663.100.2.252

Hu, C.-F., & Catts, H. W. (1998). The role of phonological processing in early reading ability: What we can learn from Chinese. *Scientific Studies of Reading, 2*(1), 55–79.

Jackson, P. (1968). *Life in classrooms.* New York: Holt, Rinehart, & Winston.

Jacobs, J. E., Lanza, S., Osgood, D. W., Eccles, J. S., & Wigfield, A. (2002). Changes in children's self-competence and values: Gender and domain differences across grades one through twelve. *Child Development, 73*(2), 509–527. doi:10.1111/1467–8624.00421

Janiuk, D. M., & Shanahan, T. (1988). Applying adult literacy practices in primary grade instruction. *Reading Teacher, 41*(9), 880–886. Retrieved from http://eric.ed.gov/?id=EJ370154.

Jeynes, W. H., & Littell, S. W. (2000). A meta-analysis of studies examining the effect of whole language instruction on the literacy of low-SES students. *Elementary School Journal, 101*(1), 21–33.

Johnston, A. M., Barnes, M. A., & Desrochers, A. (2008). Reading comprehension: Developmental processes, individual differences, and interventions. *Canadian Psychology/Psychologie Canadienne, 49*(2), 125–132. doi:10.1037/0708–5591.49.2.125

Junge, C., Cutler, A., & Hagoort, P. (2012). Electrophysiological evidence of early word learning. *Neuropsychologia, 50*(14), 3702–3712. doi:10.1016/j.neuropsychologia.2012.10.012

Justice, L. M., & Pullen, P. C. (2003). Promising interventions for promoting emergent literacy skills: Three evidence-based approaches. *Topics in Early Childhood Special Education, 113*, 99–113.

Justice, L. M., Skibbe, L., Canning, A., & Lankford, C. (2005). Preschoolers, print and storybooks: An observational study using eye movement analysis. *Journal of Research in Reading, 28*(3), 229–243. doi:10.1111/j.1467–9817.2005.00267.x

Kamil, M. (2008). How to get recreational reading to increase reading achievement. In Y. Kim, V. J. Risko, D. L. Compton, D. K. Dickinson,

M. K. Hundley, R. T. Jiménez, & D. Well Rowe (Eds.), *57th Yearbook of the National Reading Conference* (pp. 31–40). Oak Creek, WI: National Reading Conference.

Kessler, B. (2009). Statistical learning of conditional orthographic correspondences. *Writing Systems Research, 1*(1), 19–34. doi:10.1093/wsr/wsp004

Killi, C., Laurinen, L., & Marttunen, M. (2008). Students evaluating Internet sources: From versatile evaluators to uncritical readers. *Journal of Educational Computing Research, 39*(1), 75–95. Retrieved from http://baywood.metapress.com/app/home/contribution.asp?ref errer=parent&backto=issue,5,5;journal,43,193;linkingpublicationresu lts,1:300321,1.

Kintsch, W. (2012). Psychological models of reading comprehension and their implications for assessment. In J. Sabatini, E. Albro, & T. O'Reilly (Eds.), *Measuring up: Advances in how we assess reading ability* (pp. 21–37). Plymouth, UK: Rowman & Littlefield. Retrieved from http://books.google.com/books?hl=en&lr=&id=0gn9TV2CFm0C&pgis=1.

Korat, O., & Or, T. (2010). How new technology influences parent-child interaction: The case of e-book reading. *First Language, 30*(2), 139–154. doi:10.1177/0142723709359242

Korat, O., Segal-Drori, O., & Klien, P. (2009). Electronic and printed books with and without adult support as sustaining emergent literacy. *Journal of Educational Computing Research, 41*(4), 453–475. doi:10.2190/EC.41.4.d

Korat, O., & Shamir, A. (2007). Electronic books versus adult readers: Effects on children's emergent literacy as a function of social class. *Journal of Computer Assisted Learning, 23*(3), 248–259. doi:10.1111/j.1365–2729.2006.00213.x

Kush, J. C., & Watkins, M. W. (1996). Long-term stability of children's attitudes toward reading. *Journal of Educational Research, 89*(5), 315–319.

Landry, S. H., Smith, K. E., Swank, P. R., Zucker, T., Crawford, A. D., & Solari, E. F. (2012). The effects of a responsive parenting intervention on parent-child interactions during shared book reading. *Developmental Psychology, 48*(4), 969–986. doi:10.1037/a0026400

Lareau, A. (2003). *Unequal childhoods*. Berkeley: University of California Press.

Lee, J. (2014). Universal factors of student achievement in high-performing Eastern and Western countries. *Journal of Educational Psychology, 106*, 364–374.

Lepper, M. R., Greene, D., & Nisbett, R. E. (1973). Undermining children's intrinsic interest with extrinsic reward: A test of the "overjustification" hypothesis. *Journal of Personality and Social Psychology, 28*(1), 129–137. Retrieved from http://psycnet.apa.orgjournals/psp/28/1/129.

Leu, D. J., & Castek, J. (2006). What skills and strategies are characteristic of accomplished adolescent users of the Internet? Presented at the Annual Conference of the American Educational Research Association, San Francisco, CA.

Levy, B. A., Gong, Z., Hessels, S., Evans, M. A., & Jared, D. (2006). Understanding print: Early reading development and the contributions of home literacy experiences. *Journal of Experimental Child Psychology, 93*(1), 63–93. doi:10.1016/j.jecp.2005.07.003

Long, D. L., Oppy, B. J., & Seely, M. R. (1994). Individual differences in the time course of inferential processing. *Journal of Experimental Psychology: Learning, Memory, and Cognition, 20*(6), 1456–1470.

Magliano, J. P., & Millis, K. K. (2003). Assessing reading skill with a think-aloud procedure and latent semantic analysis. *Cognition and Instruction, 21*(3), 251–283.

Manguel, A. (1996). *A history of reading*. New York: Viking.

Mann, H. (1841). A lecture on the best mode of preparing and using spelling-books. Delivered before the American Institute of Instruction, August, 1841. *Common School Journal, 4*(2), 25.

Manning, M., & Lewis, M. (2010). Sustained silent reading: An update of the research. In E. H. Hiebert & D. R. Reutzel (Eds.), *Revisiting silent reading: New directions for teachers and researchers* (pp. 112–128). Newark, DE: International Reading Association.

Mares, M.-L., & Pan, Z. (2013). Effects of *Sesame Street*: A meta-analysis of children's learning in 15 countries. *Journal of Applied Developmental Psychology, 34*(3), 140–151. doi:10.1016/j.appdev.2013.01.001

Markman, E. M. (1979). Realizing that you don't understand: Elementary school children's awareness of inconsistencies. *Child Development, 50*(3), 643–655.

Margaryan, A., Littlejohn, A., & Vojt, G. (2011). Are digital natives a myth or reality? University students' use of digital technologies. *Computers & Education, 56*, 429–440.

Mashburn, A. J., Pianta, R. C., Hamre, B. K., Downer, J. T., Barbarin, O. A., Bryant, D., . . . Howes, C. (2008). Measures of classroom quality in prekindergarten and children's development of academic, language, and social skills. *Child Development, 79*(3), 732–49. doi:10.1111/j.1467–8624.2008.01154.x

Matthew, K. (1997). A comparison of the influence of interactive CD-ROM storybooks and traditional print storybooks on reading comprehension. *Journal of Research on Computing in Education, 29*, 1–13.

Mayer, M. (2010). It's not what you know, it's what you can find out. Retrieved from http://edge.org/response-detail/11973.

McKenna, M. C., Conradi, K., & Meyer, J. P. (2012). Reading attitudes of middle school students: Results of a US survey. *Reading Research Quarterly, 47*(3), 283–306. doi:10.1002/RRQ.021

McKenna, M. C., Kear, D. J., & Ellsworth, R. A. (1995). Children's attitudes toward reading: A national survey. *Reading Research Quarterly, 30*(4), 934–956.

Melby-Lervåg, M., Lyster, S.-A. H., & Hulme, C. (2012). Phonological skills and their role in learning to read: A meta-analytic review. *Psychological Bulletin, 138*(2), 322–352. doi:10.1037/a0026744

Miller, D., & Moss, B. (2013). *No more independent reading without support.* Portsmouth, NH: Heinemann.

Mills, K. L. (2014). Effects of Internet use on the adolescent brain: Despite popular claims, experimental evidence remains scarce. *Trends in Cognitive Sciences, 18*, 385–387.

Moffitt, M. A. S., & Wartella, E. (1991). Youth and reading: A survey of leisure reading pursuits of female and male adolescents. *Reading Research and Instruction, 31*(2), 1–17. doi:10.1080/19388079209558075

Mol, S. E., & Bus, A. G. (2011). To read or not to read: A meta-analysis of print exposure from infancy to early adulthood. *Psychological Bulletin, 137*(2), 267–296. doi:10.1037/a0021890

Mol, S. E., Bus, A. G., de Jong, M. T., & Smeets, D.J.H. (2008). Added value of dialogic parent-child book reading: A meta-analysis. *Early Education and Development, 19*(1), 7–26.

Morgan, P. L., & Fuchs, D. (2007). Is there a bidirectional relationship between children's reading skills and reading motivation? *Exceptional Children, 73*(2), 165–183.

Morrow, L. M. (1983). Home and school correlates of early interest in literature. *Journal of Educational Research, 76*(4), 221–230. Retrieved from http://eric.ed.gov/?id=EJ280231.

Morrow, L. M. (1992). The impact of a literature-based program on literacy achievement, use of literature, and attitudes of children from minority backgrounds. *Reading Research Quarterly, 27*(3), 250–275.

Moss, B. (2008). The information text gap: The mismatch between non-narrative text types in basal readers and 2009 NAEP recommended guidelines. *Journal of Literacy Research, 40*(2), 201–219. doi:10.1080/10862960802411927

Mueller, C. M., & Dweck, C. S. (1998). Praise for intelligence can undermine children's motivation and performance. *Journal of Personality and Social Psychology, 75*(1), 33–52. Retrieved from http://www.ncbi.nlm.nih.gov/pubmed/9686450.

National Institute of Child Health and Human Development. (2000). *Report of the National Reading Panel. Teaching children to read: (Reports of the subgroups)*. Washington, DC. Retrieved from http://www.nichd.nih.gov/research/supported/Pages/nrp.aspx/.

National Institute of Child Health and Human Development. Early Child Care Research Network. (2002). The relation of global first-grade classroom environment to structural classroom features and teacher and student behaviors. *Elementary School Journal, 102*(5), 367–387.

National Institute of Child Health and Human Development. Early Child Care Research Network. (2005). A day in third grade: A large-scale study of classroom quality and teacher and student behavior. *Elementary School Journal, 105*(3), 305–323.

National Research Council. (1998). *Preventing reading difficulties in young children.* Washington, DC: National Academies Press.

Nelson, D.G.K., Hirsh-Pasek, K., Jusczyk, P. W., & Cassidy, K. W. (1989). How the prosodic cues in motherese might assist language learning. *Journal of Child Language, 16*(01), 55–68. doi:10.1017/S030500090001343X

Neuman, S. B., Kaefer, T., Pinkham, A., & Strouse, G. (2014, February 24). Can babies learn to read? A randomized trial of baby media. *Journal of Educational Psychology, 106,* 815–830.

Neumann, M. M., Hood, M., Ford, R. M., & Neumann, D. L. (2011). The role of environmental print in emergent literacy. *Journal of Early Childhood Literacy, 12*(3), 231–258. doi:10.1177/1468798411417080

Noel Foulin, J. (2005). Why is letter-name knowledge such a good predictor of learning to read? *Reading and Writing, 18*(2), 129–155. doi:10.1007/s11145–004–5892–2

Nusername. (2013). AskReddit. *Reddit.* Retrieved from http://www.reddit.com/r/AskReddit/comments/15yaap/if_someone_from_the_1950s_suddenly_appeared_today/c7qyp13?context=5#c7qyp13.

Parise, E., & Csibra, G. (2012) Electrophysiological evidence for the understanding of maternal speech by 9-month-old infants. *Psychological Science, 23,* 728–733.

Parish-Morris, J., Mahajan, N., Hirsh-Pasek, K., & Golinkoff, R. M. (2011). Once upon a time: Parent-child dialogue and storybook reading in the electronic era. *Mind, Brain, and Education, 7*(3), 200–211.

Pashler, H. E. (1999). *The psychology of attention.* Cambridge, MA: MIT Press

Pentimonti, J. M., Zucker, T. A., Justice, L. M., & Kaderavek, J. N. (2010). Informational text use in preschool classroom read-alouds. *Reading Teacher, 63*(8), 656–665. doi:10.1598/RT.63.8.4

Piasta, S. B., & Wagner, R. K. (2010). Learning letter names and sounds: Effects of instruction, letter type, and phonological processing skill. *Journal of Experimental Child Psychology*, *105*(4), 324–344. doi:10.1016/j.jecp.2009.12.008

Pressley, M. (2002). Balanced literacy instruction. *Focus on Exceptional Children*, *34*(5), 1–14.

Rayner, K., Foorman, B. R., Perfetti, C. A., Pesetsky, D., & Seidenberg, M. S. (2001). How psychological science informs the teaching of reading. *Psychological Science*, *2*(2 Suppl.), 31–74. Retrieved from http://www.ncbi.nlm.nih.gov/pubmed/11878018.

Rayner, K., Pollatsek, A., Ashby, J., & Clifton, Charles, J. (2012). *Psychology of reading* (2nd ed.). New York: Psychology Press.

Rehm, D. (2013, October 22). Billy Collins: "Aimless love: New and selected poems." *The Diane Rehm Show*. Retrieved from http://thedianerehmshow.org/shows/2013–10–22/billy-collins-aimless-love-new-and-selected-poems/transcript.

Retelsdorf, J., Köller, O., & Möller, J. (2014). Reading achievement and reading self-concept: Testing the reciprocal effects model. *Learning and Instruction*, *29*, 21–30. doi:10.1016/j.learninstruc.2013.07.004

Richtel, M. (2012, November 1). Technology changing how students learn, teachers say. *New York Times*, p. A18.

Rideout, V. J., Foehr, U. G., & Roberts, D. F. (2010). *Generation M2: Media in the lives of 8- to 18-year-olds* (p. 79). Menlo Park, CA: Kaiser Family Foundation.

Ritchie, S. J., Bates, T. C., & Plomin, R. (2014). Does learning to read improve intelligence? A longitudinal multivariate analysis in identical twins from age 7 to 16. *Child Development*. doi:10.1111/cdev.12272.

Robinson, A. (2007). *The story of writing* (2nd ed.). London: Thames & Hudson.

Robinson, R. (2014). *Kids and family reading report* (4th ed.). Retrieved from http://mediaroom.scholastic.com/files/kfrr2013-noappendix.pdf.

Rockinson-Szapkiw, A. J., Courduff, J., Carter, K., & Bennett, D. (2013). Electronic versus traditional print textbooks: A comparison study on the influence of university students' learning. *Computers and Education*, *63*, 259–266. doi:10.1016/j.compedu.2012.11.022

Rose, J. (2006). *Independent review of the teaching of early reading: Interim report*. London: Department for Education and Skills. Retrieved from http://webarchive.nationalarchives.gov.uk/20100526143644/ http:// standards.dcsf.gov.uk/phonics/report.pdf.

Rosenshine, B., & Meister, C. (1994). Reciprocal teaching: A review of the research. *Review of Educational Research, 64*(4), 479–530.

Rosenshine, B., Meister, C., & Chapman, S. (1996). Teaching students to generate questions: A review of the intervention studies. *Review of Educational Research, 66*(2), 181–221. doi:10.3102/00346543066002181

Rosenwald, M. S. (2014, April 6). Serious reading takes a hit from online scanning and skimming, researchers say. *Washington Post*. Retrieved from http://www.washingtonpost.com/local/serious-reading-takes-a-hit-from -online-scanning-and-skimming-researchers-say/2014/04/06/088028d2 -b5d2–11e3-b899–20667de76985_story.html.

Rowe, K. J. (1991). The influence of reading activity at home on students' attitudes. *British Journal of Educational Psychology*, 19–35.

Ruble, D. N., & Frey, K. S. (1991). Changing patterns of comparative behavior as skills are acquired: A functional model of self-evaluation. In J. Suls & T. A. Wills (Eds.), *Social comparison: Contemporary theory and research* (pp. 79–113). Hillsdale, NJ: Erlbaum.

Samuels, J. (1979). The method of repeated readings. *Reading Teacher, 32*, 403–408.

Sanchez, C. A., & Wiley, J. (2009). To scroll or not to scroll: Scrolling, working memory capacity, and comprehending complex texts. *Human Factors, 51*(5), 730–738. doi:10.1177/0018720809352788

Schmitt, N., Jiang, X., & Grabe, W. (2011). The percentage of words known in a text and reading comprehension. *Modern Language Journal, 95*(1), 26–43. doi:10.1111/j.1540–4781.2011.01146.x

Schneider, W., Körkel, J., & Weinert, F. E. (1989). Domain-specific knowledge and memory performance: A comparison of high- and low-aptitude children, *81*(3), 306–312.

Schugar, J. T., Schugar, H., & Penny, C. (2011). A nook or a book? Comparing college students' reading comprehension levels, critical reading, and study skills. *International Journal of Technology in Teaching and Learning, 7*(2), 174–192.

Segal-Drori, O., Korat, O., Shamir, A., & Klein, P. S. (2009). Reading electronic and printed books with and without adult instruction: Effects on emergent reading. *Reading and Writing, 23*(8), 913–930. doi:10.1007/s11145–009–9182-x

Senechal, M., & Young, L. (2008). The effect of family literacy interventions on children's acquisition of reading from kindergarten to grade 3: A meta-analytic review. *Review of Educational Research, 78*(4), 880–907. doi:10.3102/0034654308320319

Seymour, P.H.K., Aro, M., & Erskine, J. M. (2003). Foundation literacy acquisition in European orthographies. *British Journal of Psychology, 94*(Pt. 2), 143–174. doi:10.1348/000712603321661859

Shanahan, T., & Lomax, R. G. (1986). An analysis and comparison of theoretical models of the reading–writing relationship. *Journal of Educational Psychology, 78*(2), 116–123. Retrieved from http://psycnet .apa.orgjournals/edu/78/2/116.

Shanahan, T., & Shanahan, C. (2008). Teaching disciplinary literacy to adolescents: Rethinking content-area literacy. *Harvard Educational Review, 78*(1), 40–60.

Share, D. L. (1995). Phonological recoding and self-teaching: Sine qua non of reading acquisition. *Cognition, 55*(2), 151–218; discussion 219–226. Retrieved from http://www.ncbi.nlm.nih.gov/pubmed /7789090.

Silvén, M., Niemi, P., & Voeten, M. J. (2002). Do maternal interaction and early language predict phonological awareness in 3- to 4-year-olds? *Cognitive Development, 17*(1), 1133–1155. doi:10.1016/ S0885–2014(02)00093-X

Sonnenschein, S., Stapleton, L. M., & Benson, A. (2009). The relation between the type and amount of instruction and growth in children's reading competencies. *American Educational Research Journal, 47*(2), 358–389. doi:10.3102/0002831209349215

Stabiner, A., Chasin, J., & Haver, K. (2003). *A comprehensive approach to balanced literacy: A handbook for educators.* New York: New York City Department of Education.

Stahl, S. A., & Miller, P. D. (1989). Whole language and language experience approaches for beginning reading: A quantitative research synthesis. *Review of Educational Research, 59,* 87–116.

Stanovich, K. E. (1986). Matthew effects in reading: Some consequences of individual differences in the acquisition of literacy. *Reading Research Quarterly, 21,* 360–407.

Stanovich, K. E., & Cunningham, A. E. (1993). Where does knowledge come from? Specific associations between print exposure and information acquisition. *Journal of Educational Psychology, 85*(2), 211–229. doi:10.1037//0022–0663.85.2.211

Stanovich, K. E., Cunningham, A. E., & West, R. F. (1995). Literacy experiences and the shaping of cognition, In S. G. Paris & H. M. Wellman (Eds.), *Global prospects for education: Development, culture, and schooling* (pp. 253–288). Washington, DC: American Psychological Association.

Stuart, E. W., Shimp, T. A., & Engle, R. W. (1984). Classical conditioning of consumer attitudes: Four experiments in an advertising context. *Journal of Consumer Research, 14,* 334–349.

Suggate, S. P. (2010). Why what we teach depends on when: Grade and reading intervention modality moderate effect size. *Developmental Psychology, 46*(6), 1556–1579. doi:10.1037/a0020612

Sulin, R. A., & Dooling, D. J. (1974). Intrusion of a thematic idea in retention of prose. *Journal of Experimental Psychology, 103*(2), 255–262. doi:10.1037/h0036846

Tamim, R. M., Bernard, R. M., Borokhovski, E., Abrami, P. C., & Schmid, R. F. (2011). What forty years of research says about the impact of technology on learning: A second-order meta-analysis and validation study. *Review of Educational Research, 81*(1), 4–28. doi:10.3102/0034654310393361

Tan, A., & Nicholson, T. (1997). Flashcards revisited: Training poor readers to read words faster improves their comprehension of text. *Journal of Educational Psychology, 89*(2), 276–288. doi:10.1037//0022–0663.89.2.276

Tizard, B., & Hughes, M. (1984). *Young children learning.* Cambridge, MA: Harvard University Press.

Treiman, R., & Kessler, B. (2003). The role of letter names in the acquisition of literacy. In R. Kail (Ed.), *Advances in child development and behavior* (Vol. 31, pp. 105–135). San Diego, CA: Academic Press.

Treiman, R., Kessler, B., & Pollo, T. C. (2006). Learning about the letter name subset of the vocabulary: Evidence from US and Brazilian preschoolers. *Applied Psycholinguistics, 27,* 211–227.

Treiman, R., Levin, I., & Kessler, B. (2012). Linking the shapes of alphabet letters to their sounds: The case of Hebrew. *Reading and Writing, 25*(2), 569–585. doi:10.1007/s11145–010–9286–3

Troseth, G. L., Saylor, M. M., & Archer, A. H. (2006). Young children's use of video as a source of socially relevant information. *Child Development, 77*(3), 786–799. doi:10.1111/j.1467–8624.2006.00903.x

Trushell, J., Burrell, C., & Maitland, A. (2001). Year 5 pupils reading an "interactive storybook" on CD-ROM: Losing the plot? *British Journal of Educational Technology, 32*(4), 389–401.

Vaughn, J. S. (1902, August). Our strange language. *Spectator,* 187.

Veenendaal, N. J., Groen, M. A., & Verhoeven, L. (2014). What oral text reading fluency can reveal about reading comprehension. *Journal of Research in Reading.* doi:10.1111/1467–9817.12024

Villiger, C., Niggli, A., Wandeler, C., & Kutzelmann, S. (2012). Does family make a difference? Mid-term effects of a school/home-based intervention program to enhance reading motivation. *Learning and Instruction, 22*(2), 79–91. doi:10.1016/j.learninstruc.2011.07.001

Walberg, H. J., & Tsai, S. (1985). Correlates of reading achievement and attitude: An assessment study. *Journal of Educational Research, 78*(3), 159–167.

Wallbrown, F. H., Brown, D. H., & Engin, A. W. (1978). A factor analysis of reading attitudes along with measures of reading achievement and scholastic aptitude. *Psychology in the Schools, 15*(2), 160–165. doi:10.1002/1520–6807(197804)15:2<160::AID-PITS2310150204>3.0.CO;2-G

Weizman, Z. O., & Snow, C. E. (2001). Lexical output as related to children's vocabulary acquisition: Effects of sophisticated exposure and support for meaning. *Developmental Psychology, 37*(2), 265–279. Retrieved from http://psycnet.apa.orgjournals/dev/37/2/265.

Wigfield, A., & Eccles, J. S. (2000). Expectancy-value theory of achievement motivation. *Contemporary Educational Psychology, 25,* 68–81.

Willingham, D. T. (2005). How praise can motivate—or stifle. *American Educator, 29*(4), 23–27, 48.

Willingham, D. T. (2008, summer). What is developmentally appropriate practice? *American Educator,* 34–39.

Woolfolk, M. E., Castellan, W., & Brooks, C. I. (1983). Pepsi versus Coke: Labels, not tastes, prevail. *Psychological Reports, 52,* 185–186.

Xue, Y., & Meisels, S. J. (2004). Early literacy instruction and learning in kindergarten: Evidence from the early childhood longitudinal study: Kindergarten class of 1998–1999. *American Educational Research Journal, 41*(1), 191–229.

Yoon, J. (2002). Three decades of sustained silent reading: A meta-analytic review of the effects of SSR on attitude towards reading. *Reading Improvement, 39*(4), 186–195.

Yuill, N., Oakhill, J., & Parkin, A. (1989). Working memory, comprehension ability and the resolution of text anomaly. *British Journal of Psychology, 80,* 351–361.

Zevenbergen, A. A., & Whitehurst, G. J. (2003). Dialogic reading: A shared picture book reading intervention for preschoolers. In A. van Kleeck, S. A. Stahl, & E. B. Bauer (Eds.), *On reading books to children: Parents and teachers* (pp. 177–200). Hillsdale, NJ: Erlbaum.

Zhang, S., & Duke, N. K. (2011). The impact of instruction in the WWWDOT framework on students' disposition and ability to evaluate web sites as sources of information. *Elementary School Journal, 112*(1), 132–154. doi:10.1086/660687

Ziegler, J. C., Stone, G. O., & Jacobs, A. M. (1997). What is the pronunciation for -ough and the spelling for /u /? A database for computing feedforward and feedback consistency in English. *Behavior Research Methods, Instruments, and Computers, 29*(4), 600–618.

Zimmerman, F. J., Gilkerson, J., Richards, J. A., Christakis, D. A., Xu, D., Gray, S., & Yapanel, U. (2009). Teaching by listening: The importance of adult-child conversations to language development. *Pediatrics, 124*(1), 342–349. doi:10.1542/peds.2008-2267

INDEX

Page references followed by *fig* indicate an illustrated figure.